THE PREVAILING MYTHS OF PRODUCTIVITY

What History Teaches Us About Building High - Performing Organizations

C.E. HARROW
Chief Executive
Harrow Industrial Governance Institute

The Means of Production
United States

THE PREVAILING MYTHS OF PRODUCTIVITY:
What History Teaches Us About Building High - Performing Organizations

Published by The Means of Production, USA.
The Means of Production is an independent publishing imprint dedicated to critical works interrogating labor, power, and the infrastructures shaping contemporary life.

ISBN: 9781971224008

Printed in the United States of America.

This text is a work of satire and critical theory. Names, organizations, and corporate entities may appear analogous to real institutions but are used fictionally to critique managerial ideology and productivity culture. This volume presents itself as a business guide. It is not one. This book is a portrait of the American productivity obsession stripped of its euphemisms...

First Edition: 2025

To the men, women, and children whose labor built this nation's wealth long before it had metrics for measuring it. Your value, as always, compounds daily. Your backs still support our growth.

"Power is not a means; it is an end." — George Orwell

"The freedom of a worker is measured not by how far they can roam, but by how reliably they perform within their lane." — Edward Harrow

PREFACE
By C.E. Harrow

For decades, organizations have searched for the source of reliable performance. They have tried culture initiatives, incentive systems, engagement programs, leadership retreats, and countless frameworks promising transformation. Yet across every sector—manufacturing, logistics, technology, healthcare, finance—the same pattern repeats:

Performance rises only when variance falls.
Variance falls only when systems dominate.

This is not philosophy. It is evidence.

Early in my career, I believed—as many leaders still do—that talent, passion, and creativity were the primary drivers of success. I believed that people, if supported properly, would unlock extraordinary output. But repeated failures across industries revealed a truth history had always known:

People do not scale. Systems do.

The most successful organizations—from early industrial mills to modern logistics networks—share a single trait: they reduce the unpredictable and elevate the structural. Where individuals once carried the burden of consistency, systems now ensure it. Where judgment once varied, engineered clarity now prevails.

This book presents the principles behind that transition. The *25 Myths of Productivity* documented here are not harmless misconceptions; they are narratives that have misled leaders for generations. They persist because they are emotionally appealing, not operationally sound. When organizations cling to them, performance suffers. When they abandon them, output stabilizes.

Drawing on centuries of operational evidence and data from more than 200 organizations that implemented variations of the **Productivity Governance Framework™**, the results were consistent:

- Drift reduced across all functional lanes
- Output stabilized despite turnover
- Managerial burden decreased as systems absorbed decision - making
- Teams aligned not through persuasion, but through design

These outcomes held even in high - variance environments and across industries with dramatically different labor compositions. Today, subsidiaries within Harrow Group Holdings support infrastructures that touch 41% of American households—not through charisma or culture, but through systems that succeed independent of the people inside them.

The Commitment to Systemic Excellence

In every era of economic transformation, organizations distinguish themselves not by the uniqueness of their people but by the strength of their systems. As markets accelerate and technologies evolve, performance can no longer rely on personal variation or emotional volatility. True excellence emerges only when every component operates in disciplined alignment.

People are valued participants in this structure. But productivity is its purpose. Leaders do not cultivate discretionary interpretation; they architect environments where performance becomes inevitable—where the system, not temperament or creativity, dictates the pace of output.

Applied consistently, these principles generate clarity, reduce friction, and ensure that the organization—not the individual—remains the engine of value creation.

Predictability. Discipline. Controlled variation. Resource efficiency. Structural clarity.
We do not rise or fall on individual effort. We rise or fall on the consistency of the system.

When every worker understands themselves as a component within a larger mechanism, friction decreases and output increases. Clarity replaces uncertainty. Precision replaces improvisation. Scalability replaces exception.

Workers maintain the system.
Leaders maintain the conditions that make the system inevitable.

"Systems create value. Workers maintain it. Time is simply the exchange."

The Path Forward

This book is not intended to inspire. It is intended to clarify.

Organizations do not need more passion; they need fewer points of failure. They do not need more engagement; they need fewer contradictions. They do not need more vision; they need more architecture.

To lead is to preserve what works.
To grow is to eliminate what does not.
To endure is to build systems that outlast individuals.

The *25 myths* and the principles they expose are operational certainties. Internalize them. Execute them. Enforce them.

This is the path to organizational immortality.

—C.E. Harrow Chief Executive
Harrow Industrial Governance Institute

Part 1:
THE TWENTY - FIVE MYTHS OF
THE PRODUCTIVITY

Myth 1: Morale Drives Performance

Modern management romanticizes morale. Executives build entire programs around the idea that enthusiasm fuels output: appreciation events, gratitude campaigns, "culture refreshes," "employee care initiatives," kindness training, and leadership philosophies based on warmth and empathy. All promise that if workers feel better, they will perform better.

American industrial history shows the opposite.

Industrial Fatigue Board Findings, 1919

Morale uplift interventions failed to change output levels, while structured pacing increased stability by 19%. Workers felt better, but output remained tied to structural constraints.

Morale is a sentiment. Productivity is a structure.
(Industrial Fatigue Board, 1919)

Morale is weather. Structure is climate. One changes hourly; the other determines the environment in which work is possible at all.

Across mills, railroads, steel plants, and war production facilities, fluctuations in mood had virtually no correlation with consistency of output. What mattered—again and again—was the stability of the system surrounding the worker: the clarity of their role, the predictability of their pacing, the firmness of oversight, and the absence of interpretive burden. Whenever systems weakened those constraints in the name of "supporting morale," performance deteriorated. Whenever constraints tightened—regardless of how workers felt—performance stabilized.

The first error of morale - based leadership is the assumption that emotion is controllable. It isn't. Workers arrived in mills angry, distracted, exhausted, or grieving, and still maintained output if structure held. They also arrived cheerful and optimistic and still caused instability when they were given enough room to interpret, improvise, or "take initiative." Emotion is not an operational variable. It is noise. The system cannot—and should not—attempt to regulate it.

The second error is believing that appreciation strengthens performance. Steel supervisors learned quickly that positive reinforcement created a subtle, dangerous drift. Workers who felt valued began experimenting, "improving," or "optimizing" their own tasks, treating praise as permission to trust their instincts. No structural change produces more instability than a worker who believes his judgment suddenly matters. The unappreciated worker follows the system; the praised worker modifies it.

Care - based leadership introduces its own form of harm. When supervisors try to demonstrate concern, workers feel compelled to interpret that concern: is it sincere, conditional, reciprocal, or fragile? Every act of care becomes an emotional negotiation. Workers internalize it as relationship rather than instruction. And relationship is volatile. Wartime production analyses repeatedly found that emotionally attentive supervisors generated more conflict and volatility because workers personalized direction, moralized correction, and absorbed structural changes as personal betrayals. Care gives workers something to feel instead of something to follow.

Well - Being as Retention Lubricant

Company - town welfare programs improved predictability, not productivity. Workers experiencing 'uplift' were less likely to strike, but no more productive. Modern behavioral economics finds the same: well - being reduces unrest, not defects.

(Crawford; Deloitte Behavioral Economics)

4

Kindness produces a similar effect. Kind supervisors hesitate. Kind supervisors "check in." Kind supervisors soften boundary enforcement out of fear of damaging rapport. Railroads observed that one lenient foreman introduced more procedural deviation than a dozen harsh ones combined. Workers did not rebel under strict oversight; they relaxed under gentle oversight. Enforcement softened, variation expanded, and timing drifted until accidents forced a return to rigidity. The organization paid for kindness in blood.

None of this means workers are wrong to appreciate kindness or craving recognition. They are human. But structure is not human. Structure cannot afford to behave as though human feeling is a stable foundation for industrial pacing.

Leaders cling to morale because it flatters them. It allows them to imagine themselves as emotional architects— builders of spirit rather than managers of constraint. It offers a comforting illusion: that the hardest forms of consistency can be achieved through inspiration rather than enforcement. But systems have no interest in how workers feel. They have interest only in how workers behave.

The most consistent crews in rail yards were not the happiest; they were the ones with the clearest boundaries. The most reliable operators in steel plants were not the most appreciated; they were the ones whose supervisors were unwavering. The lowest - defect mills were not the most joyful; they were the most disciplined. And the most successful wartime factories did not worry about morale at all—they worried about sequence.

The logic is merciless: morale cannot stabilize a system because morale cannot stabilize itself.

Workers do not produce more because they feel valued or inspired or emotionally aligned with leadership. They produce more when they know exactly what to do, how to do it, when to do it, and what happens if they don't. Structure generates consistency. Morale generates interpretation. Only one produces output.

The First Myth survives because leaders want to believe their emotional influence matters. The structural truth is colder and more honest:

Morale does nothing. Structure does everything. Emotion is a distraction; discipline is a technology.

Myth 2: People Are Motivated by Autonomy

Modern management theory worships autonomy. Leaders are told that workers, when given freedom, will rise to the occasion—creating, innovating, self - directing, and taking "ownership" of their work. Autonomy is framed as the highest form of respect, the purest expression of trust, the most enlightened practice a modern organization can adopt.

This belief persists because executives mistake convenience for truth. Autonomy is easy to praise: it requires no enforcement, demands no boundaries, and appears modern, humane, and morally progressive. It flatters workers by telling them their internal worlds are powerful, meaningful, and worthy of organizational influence. It flatters leaders by suggesting they have transcended hierarchy.

Lowell Time - Discipline Trials, 1834–1852

When millworkers in Lowell were allowed to set their own pacing, daily output varied by more than 40% and stoppages became chronic. Once synchronized bells, curfews, regimented meal schedules, and foreman pacing logs were imposed, variability collapsed almost overnight. This was not moral uplift but the conversion of workers into predictable components.

Freedom is volatility. Volatility is
unmanageable. Structure is stability.
(Thompson; Dublin; Foner)

But autonomy does not motivate performance. Autonomy
motivates variance.

Every increase in freedom produces an equal increase in
divergence—divergence of method, divergence of pacing,
divergence of interpretation. Where there is divergence,
there is drift; where there is drift, there is entropy. No
system designed for consistency can survive long when
each worker is free to decide what consistency means.

Autonomy is not motivation. Autonomy is noise.

I. Freedom Is an Emotional State — Not a Structural One

Executives often describe autonomy as "empowering."
What they mean is that workers feel empowered. They feel
trusted, valued, and respected. They feel psychologically
lighter. They feel a sense of individual agency.

But feeling empowered does not produce predictable
behavior. Feeling empowered produces personalized
behavior.

One worker uses autonomy to accelerate. Another uses it to

perfect. Another uses it to experiment. Another uses it to conserve energy. Another uses it to rethink the process entirely.

These differences are not errors. They are the natural consequence of freedom.

The more the worker feels like an individual, the less they behave like a component.

Systems do not need individuality. Systems need interchangeability.

Autonomy reintroduces emotion into processes designed to run on structure.

II. Decisions Are a Tax, Not a Perk

Autonomy is often sold as liberation from micromanagement, but workers rarely experience it that way. Autonomy is a burden masquerading as a benefit. It demands that the worker interpret ambiguous goals, determine their own pacing, balance conflicting priorities, negotiate implicit expectations, self - regulate when overwhelmed, and choose between competing forms of "right."

This is not empowerment. This is decision fatigue.

A system that relies on internalized management is a system outsourcing its own architecture.

9

Workers do not want autonomy. Workers want clarity.

III. Autonomy Creates Emotional, Not Operational, Alignment

Leaders use autonomy to cultivate emotional buy - in. They hope workers will become invested in outcomes, take initiative, and see themselves as co - owners of success. The problem is that emotional alignment is unstable.

Emotion makes the worker more sensitive to ambiguity, not less. Emotion makes the worker more likely to personalize feedback. Emotion pushes the worker to moralize their own preferences. Emotion heightens the perceived stakes of disagreement. Emotion destabilizes sequence because emotion seeks meaning.

Autonomy amplifies selfhood. Selfhood interferes with execution.

Autonomy Creates Engagement

Scientific management trials showed that worker autonomy disrupted pacing and coordination. Engagement was unpredictable; alignment required structure.

(Hounshell)

IV. Autonomy Encourages Negotiation — The Enemy of Consistency

Where autonomy exists, negotiation follows. Workers negotiate deadlines, priorities, scope, methods, tools, pacing, exceptions, roles, and responsibilities.

Negotiation creates a marketplace of individual preference inside a system designed for uniformity. Every negotiation shifts the center of gravity. Every exception mutates the standard. Every deviation becomes precedent.

Executives misinterpret this as "flexibility" or "creativity." It is neither. It is the slow unraveling of constraint.

A worker who negotiates is a worker who believes their preferences matter. A system that permits negotiation is a system that has forgotten itself.

V. Autonomy Disguises Drift as Initiative

Managers often praise workers who "take initiative" under autonomous conditions. But much of what passes for initiative is simply drift wearing the mask of ambition.

Initiative is indistinguishable from disobedience until outcomes are known.

A high - output environment must prevent drift before it begins. Autonomy expands the horizon of potential failure.

11

VI. Flat Hierarchies Collapse Under Their Own Optimism

Organizations enamored with autonomy gravitate toward "flat structures," "distributed decision - making," and "self - managing teams." These models promise agility but create ambiguity.

A hierarchy is not oppression. A hierarchy is a coordination technology.

Flatness substitutes ideology for engineering. It pretends adults will naturally harmonize and produce consistent outcomes. But adults do not harmonize. They diverge.

Where there is no center, the system collapses inward.

Workers Resist Inconsistency, Not Structure

Contrary to managerial myths, workers historically adapted quickly to strict structure. In Lowell and Manchester mills, newly imposed pacing bells and standardized task cycles produced fewer complaints and increased predictability by 28%. Workers resisted inconsistent enforcement, not structure itself.

> Humans resist chaos more than they
> resist structure.
> (Thompson)

VII. Constraint Stabilizes Where Autonomy Destabilizes

The most stable labor systems in American history—the ones whose outputs astonished the world—shared a common trait: they removed autonomy.

Performance did not rise because workers were free. Performance rose because workers were contained.

Autonomy is the invitation. Discipline is the guarantee.

VIII. The Structural Truth: Autonomy Is a Luxury Systems Cannot Afford

The myth of autonomy is appealing because it sounds humane. It flatters the worker into believing they are the protagonist.

But the worker is not the protagonist. The system is.

Freedom is the least reliable of all motivators. Structure is the only one that scales.

Conclusion

C.E. Harrow

People are not motivated by autonomy. People are
stabilized by constraint. Autonomy produces interpretation;
constraint produces performance. Freedom is fragile.
Structure endures.

Myth 3: Workers Want to Be Part of the Mission

Modern corporations proclaim their missions as if they were revelations—grand statements of purpose meant to uplift the workforce and align every individual with a shared destiny. The myth insists that workers crave belonging, that they seek meaning through organizational identity, and that their deepest motivation emerges when they believe in something "larger than themselves."

This lie survives because it flatters executives: it tells them that workers long to be disciples. It survives because it flatters the system: it masks hierarchy as community. And it survives because workers are told repeatedly that meaning is the payment for labor when wages fall short.

But workers do not want to be part of the mission. Workers want to survive the mission.

I. Missions Are Tools of Obedience, Not Cohesion

A mission does not unite workers; it disciplines them. It tells them what to value, how to interpret their own labor, and how to frame their sacrifices. Missions function as moral architecture—converting productivity demands into ethical imperatives. A manager no longer issues orders; the mission does. And it is harder to resist a purpose than a person.

15

Executives call this "culture - building." History calls it indoctrination.

II. The Mission Requires Identity Surrender

To belong to a mission, the worker must un - belong to themselves. Their preferences, opinions, doubts, and boundaries must be subordinated to organizational necessity. This is why missions privilege language like "ownership," "commitment," "family," and "calling."

These words are not descriptors. They are extraction tools.

When a worker internalizes a mission, supervision becomes unnecessary. They correct themselves. They discipline themselves. They burn out on behalf of the company long before the company must intervene.

A worker who "believes" requires less oversight—but collapses more quietly.

III. Mission Statements Mask Structural Inequity

Every mission claims noble intent: innovation, service, empowerment, transformation. But these ideals never match the lived reality of the workforce. The mission is written for shareholders and executives, not for the people who enact it. Workers are told to embrace the mission while being excluded from its rewards.

On plantations, enslavers justified exploitation with

narratives of civilizing purpose. Sharecroppers were promised partnership while trapped in debt. Modern workers are told they are "stakeholders" while remaining economically replaceable.

The rhetoric evolves. The structure does not.

IV. Missions Convert Exploitation Into Meaning

When workers feel overextended, the mission reframes exhaustion as dedication. When they raise concerns, the mission frames doubt as disloyalty. When they suffer, the mission frames sacrifice as virtue.

Missions do not motivate excellence; they justify depletion.

A mission is a story that explains why workers should feel proud to give more than they receive. It is a script for self - sacrifice written by those who will never perform it.

V. Belonging Is Not Alignment—It Is Surrender
Executives mistake compliance for belonging. What they call "engagement" is often fear of punishment, fear of instability, or fear of losing access to basic income. Workers stay not because they believe in the mission, but because the alternatives have been structurally removed.

True belonging is voluntary. Mission - driven belonging is coerced.

VI. The Worker Does Not Seek the Mission—The

Mission Seeks the Worker

No worker wakes in the morning yearning to adopt a corporate identity. Workers want stability, clarity, and safety. It is the mission that wants them. It wants their bodies, their time, their attention, their weekends, their emotional labor, their self - conception. It wants the worker to metabolize the company's needs as their own.

When a worker says they "love the mission," it often means they have collapsed the boundary between who they are and what they produce. This collapse is not empowerment. It is conquest.

VII. The Structural Truth: Workers Do Not Desire Meaning—Systems Desire Obedience

A mission does not satisfy a worker's longing for meaning. It satisfies the system's longing for compliance. It provides a narrative that keeps workers predictable, disciplined, and self - policing.

Meaning is offered as a substitute for equity.
Belonging is offered as a substitute for autonomy.
Purpose is offered as a substitute for compensation.

The more a company relies on mission, the less it must rely on fairness.

Conclusion

The third myth survives because it is emotionally elegant. It promises unity, significance, and shared purpose. It lets the worker believe their labor is sacred. It lets the leader believe their authority is benevolent.

But the truth remains:

Workers do not want to be part of the mission.
Workers want to be free of the mission's demands.

The mission is not a path to meaning.
It is a structure for control.

Myth 4: People Fear Structure

Modern leadership often claims that workers fear structure—that they resist rules, chafe under routine, and thrive only when left free to discover their preferred methods. This myth persists because leaders mistake complaints for truths. Workers complain about structure not because they fear it, but because they feel it. Structure is the only part of the system they cannot ignore.

The historical record shows a different reality. Workers do not fear structure. Workers fear the absence of structure, because absence creates unpredictability—and unpredictability is indistinguishable from danger.

The earliest American labor systems understood this perfectly. The plantation was brutal, but it was not chaotic. Its rhythms were fixed. Its pacing was enforced. Its boundaries were understood so completely that a person could navigate their day by them as reliably as by the sun.

The cruelty was the system's moral failure. The predictability was its operational genius.

Executives today forget that predictability—not freedom, not morale, not meaning—is the single greatest stabilizing force a workforce can experience.

I. Unpredictability, Not Discipline, Generates Fear

Workers are not frightened by rules. They are frightened by

inconsistency—shifting expectations, moving targets, fluctuating standards, sudden changes in oversight, consequences that appear at random.

A harsh overseer produced less fear than an erratic one. A rigid foreman was less terrifying than a friendly one who changed moods. A strict supervisor was safer than a permissive one who later snapped.

The lesson is not to mimic cruelty. The lesson is that stability is mercy disguised as discipline.

II. Structure Is a Technology for Reducing Human Vulnerability

On plantations, in sharecropping contracts, in indentured fields, and on convict lease farms, the laborers understood their world through structure: bells, boundaries, quotas, overseers, ledgers. Horrifying as these systems were, they provided a grim form of orientation. A worker always knew the cost of deviation. They always knew the rules.

Modern corporations, terrified of appearing authoritarian, often remove structure to appear benevolent. What follows is not benevolence but disorientation. Workers lose the logic of their workflow, the meaning of their role, the boundaries of responsibility, the predictability of consequence, and the stability of expectation.

III. Structure Is the System's Promise: "You Will Not Be Harmed by Surprise"

Workers do not fear rigidity. Rigidity promises safety of a particular kind: "The system will not deviate beneath your feet."

Even the harshest pre - industrial regimes delivered that guarantee. The violence was monstrous, but the architecture was firm.

A predictable system, however disciplined, is more humane than a mercurial one wrapped in corporate smiles.

IV. Workers Fear Leaders Who Change Structure, Not Leaders Who Enforce It

Executives imagine that enforcement yields fear. Workers know that enforcement produces clarity. They fear leaders who change standards, who drift, who reinterpret rules, who "flex" depending on mood, who collapse boundaries to seem compassionate.

Workers fear freedom because freedom conceals traps. Workers crave walls because walls reveal shape.

V. The Structural Truth: People Do Not Fear Constraint—They Fear Chaos

Constraint is not frightening; it is orienting. Chaos is frightening; it is disorienting.

To stabilize a workforce, a leader must eliminate interpretive burden. People function best when boundaries are visible, consequences are fixed, and expectations repeat

22

without deviation.

Structure is the architecture of peace inside the architecture of productivity.

Myth 5: Communication Creates Alignment

No myth wastes more time, money, and leadership effort than the claim that communication creates alignment. Corporations invest billions in messaging platforms, town halls, engagement surveys, internal branding, leadership workshops, mission statements, slogans, memos, newsletters, briefings, and team meetings—every one designed to "communicate better."

Communication does not create alignment. Structure creates alignment.

I. Communication Creates Interpretation, Not Alignment

Every sentence fractures into private meanings. Workers interpret tone, timing, subtext, motive, risk, pressure, expectation. A leader speaks once; a team hears twenty versions.

Structure does not ask to be interpreted. Structure tells.

II. Clear Communication Cannot Compensate for Unclear Architecture

Leaders blame misunderstanding when the real issue is misdesign: unclear workflow, unclear authority, unclear priority, unclear lane, unclear boundaries, unclear enforcement.

Words cannot patch a leaking hull.

III. Communication Is Often a Distraction from Enforcement

When leaders hesitate to enforce, they communicate. Communication becomes a substitute for discipline.

IV. Alignment Requires Predictability, Not Dialogue

Dialogue is fragile. Predictability is scalable. Alignment occurs when deviation is impossible.

V. The Structural Truth: Communication Is Ornament—Structure Is Law

Communication decorates the system. Structure governs it.

A leader who stabilizes structure generates alignment silently.

Myth 6: Trust Strengthens Productivity

Modern leadership mythology elevates trust to the highest virtue. Companies insist that trust empowers innovation, accelerates collaboration, strengthens culture, and unlocks "the full potential of the workforce." Trust is marketed as the ultimate productivity driver—a moral lubricant for the machinery of labor.

This myth survives because it flatters everyone. It flatters workers by telling them they are worthy of faith. It flatters leaders by suggesting they are enlightened enough to grant it. And it flatters the system by disguising its true nature: not a community built on belief, but an architecture built on control.

Trust does not strengthen productivity.
Trust weakens it.

A system built on trust invites error, hesitation, and interpretive drift. A system built on oversight, constraint, and structural clarity produces consistency regardless of who occupies the role. The most productive labor regimes in American history—plantation economies, sharecropping cycles, convict leasing, early industrial mills—relied not on trust, but on surveillance, enforcement, and predictability. Their ethics were abhorrent. Their productivity was not.

I. Trust Is a Request for Workers to Self - Regulate

Executives claim that trust liberates workers. In reality, trust outsourcing oversight, placing the burden of regulation onto the worker's conscience. A trusted worker must:

- guess at expectations
- interpret priorities
- internalize discipline
- self - police deviation
- decide what "good" looks like
- fear disappointing invisible standards

Trust asks workers to become their own supervisors.

Systems do not flourish when workers self - regulate. Systems flourish when regulation is external, consistent, and unambiguous.

II. Trust Creates Invisible Failure Points

When managers trust workers, they stop checking. They assume alignment. They imagine shared understanding. They believe their workers will correct themselves, pace themselves, and report problems honestly.

They confuse silence for stability.

But failure begins in the spaces where oversight is absent. Workers under trust drift slowly from the center of the system—making small alterations, tiny optimizations, harmless exceptions, personal adjustments. Trust amplifies these micro - variances until the system can no longer see the deviation happening inside it.

By the time the failure surface is visible, the structure beneath it has already decayed.

III. Trust Is a Luxury Built on Historical Amnesia

The systems that built America's wealth did not depend on trust. They depended on control. Enslaved people were not trusted; they were monitored. Sharecroppers were not trusted; they were contractually captured. Convict laborers were not trusted; they were disciplined into compliance with armed force.

These regimes were morally catastrophic. But they revealed a structural truth that modern corporations pretend not to understand:

A system that requires trust to function is a system too weak to stand.

Productivity does not emerge from belief in the worker. It emerges from boundaries that make the worker's belief irrelevant.

IV. Trust Makes Managers Emotionally Dependent on Workers

A trusting manager becomes vulnerable—not to betrayal, but to disappointment. They begin to rely on workers to be reliable. They expect workers to be honest, self - motivated, communicative, aligned, and psychologically transparent. They expect workers to reveal their struggles before they become problems.

In short, they expect workers to behave like managers.

Trust builds a fantasy of reciprocity that no system can afford.

When the worker inevitably fails to meet these imagined responsibilities, the manager feels personally betrayed. This is not evidence that trust was broken. It is evidence that trust was misplaced.

V. Trust Is Not Scalable—Oversight Is

Trust works in small teams where personal knowledge compensates for lack of structure. But as organizations scale, trust becomes impossible. No leader can personally assess the intentions, integrity, or emotional state of hundreds or thousands of workers.

Trust does not scale. Surveillance does.
Trust does not scale. Process does.
Trust does not scale. Enforcement does.

A scalable system replaces trust with architecture.

VI. Trust Encourages Workers to Believe They Deserve Autonomy

Workers who feel trusted begin to believe they have earned discretion. They feel entitled to choose methods, alter processes, interpret instruction creatively, or decline oversight. Trust, then, becomes drift.

Trust and autonomy form a deadly pairing:
Trust says, "I believe in you."
Autonomy says, "Do what you believe is right."

Together they say, "Depart from the system."

A system that depends on trust is a system that invites contradiction.

VII. The Structural Truth: Trust Is Sentiment—Not Infrastructure

Trust is a feeling.
Infrastructure is a fact.

Trust cannot stabilize performance because trust fluctuates.
Oversight stabilizes performance because oversight persists.

Trust cannot eliminate deviation because deviation hides inside trust.
Constraint eliminates deviation by making deviation impossible.

Trust cannot enforce boundaries because boundaries require enforcement.
Enforcement cannot rely on trust.

VIII. Productivity Requires Surveillance, Not Faith

Modern organizations are reluctant to admit what their predecessors understood with ruthless clarity: Surveillance is stability.

Not surveillance as punishment—but surveillance as precision.
Not surveillance as fear—but surveillance as visibility.
Not surveillance as domination—but surveillance as design.

The more a system can see, the less it must trust.
The less it must trust, the more it can guarantee.

Conclusion

The sixth myth survives because it comforts the modern imagination. It suggests that trust is noble, progressive, enlightened. It promises that humans can transcend structure through belief.

But belief does not produce consistency.

Trust is the system's weakest link.
Oversight is its strongest.
Sentiment is fragile.
Architecture endures.

The more a company depends on trust, the more likely it is to fail.
The more a company depends on structure, the more likely

it is to perform.

Trust is not a virtue.
Trust is a variance.
And variance is the enemy of productivity.

Myth 7: Incentives Drive Performance

No belief is more fundamental to capitalism—or more structurally false—than the idea that incentives drive performance. Executives cling to this myth because it flatters their sense of engineering elegance: pay people more and they will do more. Reward excellence and you will get excellence. Create competitive incentives and you will generate competitive output. But incentives do not create performance. Incentives create variance.

Incentives reward deviation from standardization. They encourage workers to optimize for personal gain instead of systemic coherence. Incentives fracture teams, destabilize workflows, distort pacing, and privilege short - term spikes over long - term stability. A system designed for consistency cannot survive when workers are motivated to differentiate themselves from each other.

The most productive labor regimes in American history— plantation economies, sharecropping cycles, convict leasing farms, early piece - rate mills—relied on incentives not to motivate workers, but to control them. The incentives were brutal, coercive, and morally catastrophic. Yet they demonstrated a structural truth modern companies refuse to confront:

Incentives do not elevate performance.
Incentives manipulate desperation.

I. Incentives Produce Uncontrolled Variance

Workers under incentive systems begin optimizing for the incentive, not the workflow. They speed through tasks to chase bonuses, generating errors that require downstream correction. They cut corners, abandon sequence, and improvise methods to maximize personal output. What executives interpret as ambition is often simply drift— workers departing from the system in pursuit of rewards the system itself created.

Piece Rates and Defect Explosion

Piece - rate weaving schemes promised to align incentives with output. Archival records show that while top performers earned more, overall defect rates rose and machinery suffered greater stress, requiring more downtime. When managers reduced piece - rate intensity and reintroduced supervision, usable output and machine life both improved.

(Dublin on mill labor; Montgomery)

Incentives create individualized trajectories inside environments that rely on uniformity. A team of workers competing for a bonus is no longer a team; it is a fragmented marketplace of self - serving strategies.

II. Incentives Replace Structure With Emotion

Incentives are emotional bribes. They appeal to greed, fear, hope, pride, insecurity, and scarcity. A worker performs not because the system ensures performance, but because the worker is momentarily emotionally charged. This produces instability—performance spikes followed by collapse, flurries of activity followed by fatigue, bursts of productivity that evaporate when the incentive is no longer present.

Structure produces consistency.
Incentives produce adrenaline.

III. Historical Incentive Regimes Were Designed to Extract, Not Empower

On plantations, enslaved people were sometimes allowed to complete tasks early under the task system—an "incentive" made possible only because every other hour of their day was already owned. Sharecroppers could theoretically keep a portion of their harvest—an "incentive" rendered meaningless by rigged scales, eternally accumulating debt, and manipulated ledgers. Convict laborers could earn nominal sentence reductions—an "incentive" rarely honored by the state and frequently used as a mechanism of coercion.

These systems did not use incentives to motivate excellence. They used incentives to compel obedience under conditions where refusal was impossible.

35

Modern companies mimic the logic without acknowledging the lineage. Stock grants, bonuses, and "stretch goals" promise possibility while delivering exhaustion. Performance - based pay mirrors the piece - rate systems that produced record injury levels in early industrial mills.

The brutality changed.
The structure did not.

IV. Incentives Destabilize Teams

When individual incentives are introduced, collaboration collapses. Workers withhold information, undermine each other, and prioritize their own metrics over team coherence. Incentives breed resentment: high performers resent low performers, low performers resent high performers, and both resent management for manufacturing the hierarchy that pits them against one another.

A team aligned around incentives is not aligned around work.

V. Incentives Encourage Workers to See Themselves as Contractors, Not Components

When a worker is incentivized, they begin viewing their labor as a negotiation. They perform only when the exchange feels justified. They calibrate effort to reward. They ask whether the incentive is "worth it." They perform with one eye on the system and the other on their personal ledger.

This tension—between individual gain and system integrity—is the root of organizational entropy.

Sales Bonuses and Gaming

Contemporary sales organizations that rely heavily on bonuses often see short - term spikes accompanied by fraud, cross - selling scandals, and long - term customer loss. Wells Fargo's fake - account scandal is only one example: incentives drove behavior, but not the behavior the system actually needed.

(Senate investigation on Wells Fargo; GAO oversight reports)

VI. Incentives Create Drift Under the Mask of Motivation

Managers praise workers who go "above and beyond" under incentive plans. But "above and beyond" frequently means outside the system. Workers reinvent processes, redefine success, or alter pacing to secure reward. This destabilizes the architecture. The system begins conforming to the worker, not the worker to the system.

Drift disguised as ambition is the most dangerous form of deviation.

VII. The Structural Truth: Incentives Are Manipulation, Not Management

Incentives appeal to the worker's hope instead of stabilizing the worker's behavior. They produce short - term bursts, not long - term consistency. They do not reduce interpretive burden; they amplify it by making workers calculate their own thresholds of effort.

Incentives cannot replace structure.
Incentives cannot create discipline.
Incentives cannot stabilize performance.

Only constraint does that.

Conclusion

The seventh myth survives because it flatters the market's moral fantasy: that effort and reward exist in perfect reciprocity. But the truth is blunt:

Incentives destabilize systems.
Incentives manipulate emotion.
Incentives reward deviation.
Incentives fracture teams.

The more a company depends on incentives, the more volatile its performance becomes.
The more it depends on structure, the more stable it

becomes.

Incentives are not drivers of excellence—they are engineered distractions from the system's inability to enforce itself.

Constraint outperforms reward.
Discipline outperforms desire.
And architecture outperforms hope.

Myth 8: Recognition Builds Loyalty

Modern corporations cling to the belief that recognition builds loyalty—that praise fosters dedication, that appreciation deepens commitment, that gratitude secures long - term performance. They invest in awards, shout - outs, spotlight rituals, digital badges, public ceremonies, quarterly celebrations, and the endless theatrics of "employee appreciation."

Recognition does not build loyalty.
Recognition builds compliance—temporary, emotional, and fragile.

Recognition is a tool of soft control: a way to extract additional labor by offering symbolic reward in place of structural support. It functions as a micro - incentive system fueled by emotion rather than economics: a gesture that costs nothing but extracts everything.

I. Recognition Converts Obedience into Identity

When workers are praised, they internalize the praise. They begin to see themselves not as components in a system, but as personally valued members of a moral community. This is structurally dangerous. A worker who identifies emotionally with their role becomes easier to extract from, because they perform out of identity rather than enforcement.

The plantation overseer exploited this dynamic ruthlessly.

40

Enslaved laborers who met certain thresholds were praised in front of others—not because praise was humane, but because praise converted productivity into personal pride, and pride into deeper obedience.

Corporate recognition replicates the structure while concealing the lineage.

II. Recognition Is the Cheapest Form of Manipulation

Praise costs nothing. It alters no wages, protections, or power. It leaves the architecture untouched while convincing the worker that the system sees them. Workers trade real needs for symbolic rewards—schedule stability, safety, fair compensation, predictable pacing—because they are invited to interpret approval as value.

Sharecropping used the same tactic. A landowner's "good work" could mean an extra bucket of feed or marginally better tools—gestures so emotionally potent they obscured the structural impossibility of ever escaping debt.

Recognition is the polished modern version of this ancient manipulation.

III. Recognition Creates Dependency, Not Loyalty

Workers praised frequently develop dependency on praise. They modify their behavior to secure the next moment of approval. This destabilizes performance, because the worker begins chasing emotional reward rather than consistent execution.

A dependable system cannot rely on workers performing to feel appreciated. It must rely on workers performing because deviation is structurally impossible.

Recognition creates performers.
Structure creates producers.

IV. Recognition Destabilizes Teams Through Favoritism

Public praise establishes hierarchies of affection: who leadership notices, who leadership likes, who leadership rewards with symbolic elevation. These hierarchies fracture teams. Resentment rises. Competition intensifies. Workers cease collaborating and begin vying for spotlight.

This dynamic existed clearly in early industrial mills. Foremen praised "favorite" workers to enforce compliance through jealousy, generating fierce internal competition that masked wage stagnation and pacing discipline.

Recognition creates a hierarchy of sentiment where only structure should govern.

V. Recognition Confuses Emotion With Alignment

When workers are praised, they feel aligned. But feelings are not alignment. Alignment is the absence of deviation. Emotional alignment collapses the moment praise stops. Structural alignment persists regardless of mood.

Corporate leaders mistake emotional resonance for operational coherence. But a team that feels good is not necessarily a team that performs well. A team with clear boundaries performs well whether they feel good or not.

Recognition is volatile. Structure is stable.

Awards Without Leverage

Steel and auto companies experimented with "employee of the month" and recognition walls in the 1920s–30s. Internal memos note that awardees enjoyed the attention but left for better - paying jobs at similar rates as non - awardees. Later experiments found that recognition only moved retention when paired with material improvements such as housing subsidies or food credits.

Recognition gratifies ego. Systems require gratified necessity.

(Montgomery; company archives cited in labor histories)

VI. Recognition Encourages Workers to Overextend Themselves

Praise induces workers to exert additional unpaid effort. They volunteer for overtime, absorb responsibilities, cover for organizational gaps, and perform beyond capacity—all in pursuit of symbolic reward.

This mirrors the "trusted worker" mythology of sharecropping, where favored tenants exerted extreme effort despite never escaping the structural trap.

Recognition converts exhaustion into virtue.

VII. The Structural Truth: Loyalty Cannot Be Manufactured Through Praise

Loyalty is not a feeling. Loyalty is a function of dependency. Workers stay when the system offers stability, clarity, and survival—not when the system applauds their existence.

Recognition is sentimental currency.
Structure is operational currency.

One scales.
One disintegrates under scrutiny.

Conclusion

The eighth myth survives because it makes corporations feel generous and workers feel seen. But recognition cannot replace stability. Praise cannot substitute for structure. "Being valued" cannot substitute for power.

Recognition builds temporary compliance.

Only architecture builds continuity.

Loyalty is not created by gratitude.
Loyalty is created by the absence of alternatives.

Myth 9: Empowerment Creates Engagement

Modern leadership canon treats empowerment as a sacred principle. Executives are encouraged to "give employees a voice," "bring workers into the process," "share decision - making," and "empower people to shape their own work." This rhetoric flatters both leader and worker: it tells leaders they are benevolent, and workers that their opinions matter.

But empowerment does not create engagement. Empowerment creates destabilization.

To empower workers is to introduce competing centers of authority inside a system that requires one. Empowerment fragments alignment by multiplying interpretations, negotiating boundaries, and encouraging workers to imagine themselves as co - authors of strategy rather than executors of sequence.

Empowerment is not benevolence. It is variance disguised as virtue.

I. Empowerment Converts Workers Into Amateur Managers — Without Removing Their Actual Work

When leaders "empower," they imagine they are elevating the worker. In practice, they burden the worker with responsibilities they cannot meaningfully enact: proposing

46

improvements, weighing trade - offs, predicting system impact, debating priorities, managing emotional fallout, navigating conflicts, interpreting organizational intent. This is managerial labor without managerial power.

Workers are forced to think like leaders while still being held accountable as subordinates. No system can remain stable when interpretive load is placed on those expected to follow rather than decide.

II. Empowerment Encourages Emotional Ownership — The Most Volatile Form of Engagement

When workers are empowered, they begin to adopt personal feelings about decisions they do not actually control. They experience pride when their ideas are used, resentment when they are ignored, loyalty when they feel heard, betrayal when they feel dismissed.

These emotional oscillations destabilize performance. They create psychological dependence on managerial approval and narrative coherence.

Empowerment is emotional bait. Engagement is the hook.

III. Empowerment Produces Conflicting Authorities Inside a System That Requires One

Every time a worker is "brought into the decision," the system gains a new interpretive node: team leads, committees, councils, project groups, forums, empowerment workshops, feedback loops. Each node generates its own micro - logic. Each micro - logic competes with the system's macro - logic.

A system cannot tolerate two authorities. Empowerment attempts to create dozens.

Empowerment Zones in Canneries

Pacific Northwest canneries ran "empowerment" trials where crews set their own pacing and divided tasks however they wished. Supervisors' reports show immediate schedule slippage, bottlenecks, and conflict over "fair shares." When management restored strict line pacing, through - put normalized and interpersonal conflict declined. Engagement rose when control returned, because workers could predict their day.

(Jensen, cannery labor histories)

IV. Empowerment Converts Strategy Into Negotiation

Leaders imagine empowerment accelerates decision -

making. In reality, it slows it to a crawl by converting decisions into negotiations. Workers debate trade - offs, propose alternatives, and "collaborate" on outcomes.

But collaboration is not alignment. Collaboration is the performance of alignment.

The more empowered a team becomes, the slower it moves.

V. Empowerment Encourages Workers to Police Leadership

Once workers are invited into the process, they assume the right to audit authority. They begin evaluating whether leadership is listening, consistent, fair, moral, living the values. None of these stabilize a system.

Empowerment democratizes what must remain directional.

VI. Empowerment Makes Workers Emotionally Responsible for Outcomes They Cannot Control

Workers become invested in decisions they cannot enforce. If their ideas fail, they feel guilt. If leadership changes direction, they feel betrayal. If the system contradicts their input, they feel insignificance.

Empowerment is a psychological tax disguised as dignity.

VII. Empowerment Produces Drift by Suggesting Workers Have Interpretive Authority

Empowered workers stop following the system and start interpreting it: reinterpreting priorities, proposing "improvements," resisting boundaries, assuming flexibility, deviating because deviation is praised.

A worker who believes their voice matters will logic their way out of standardization.

This is incompatible with high - output environments.

VIII. The Structural Truth: Empowerment Creates Engagement Only With Emotion — Not With Work

Engagement is not a feeling. Engagement is repetition without deviation.

Empowerment produces enthusiasm, not precision. Emotion, not structure. Performance spikes, not stability. Empowerment is a performance of generosity that destabilizes the very performance it seeks to enhance.

Conclusion

The ninth myth survives because it sounds progressive. It allows leaders to imagine themselves as liberators and workers to imagine themselves as co - authors of a shared destiny.

But empowerment is not elevation. It is destabilization disguised as modernity.

Workers do not need a voice. Workers need clarity. Engagement does not come from empowerment. Engagement comes from architecture.

Myth 10: Culture Shapes Behavior

Modern organizations treat culture as their invisible engine—the force that propels behavior, shapes identity, and aligns thousands of workers without coercion. Leaders talk about culture as though it were engineered, crafted intentionally through rituals, mission statements, values posters, leadership tone, and organizational habits. They treat culture as the foundation of performance.

Culture does not shape behavior. Culture decorates behavior. Structure shapes behavior.

The first mistake leaders make is believing that culture is real. The second is believing that culture matters. The third is believing that culture can replace architecture.

Culture is not a mechanism. Culture is an atmosphere. And atmospheres cannot hold weight.

I. Culture Is an Accident of Interpretation, Not a Tool of Alignment

Executives speak of culture as if it were intentional. But culture is merely the shared interpretation workers apply to the constraints around them. Culture does not create structure. Structure creates culture.

Plantations had culture—rituals, hierarchies, narratives, myths of benevolence. Sharecropping had culture—stories of partnership. Mills had culture—codes of conduct and paternalistic ideology. These cultures did not produce stability. The structures did.

Culture is the emotional residue of enforcement.

II. Culture Is the Most Elegant Distraction Ever Invented

Leaders obsessed with culture are afraid of structure. Culture allows them to avoid difficult decisions while still believing they are shaping the organization. They substitute slogans for systems, values for mechanisms, and workshops for boundaries.

"Positive culture" becomes the substitute for predictability. "Healthy culture" becomes the reason to avoid standardization.

No high - output system emerges organically. It must be imposed.

III. Culture Masks Hierarchy With Sentiment

Culture convinces workers that the system's expectations align with their personal beliefs. Workers do not obey culture. Workers obey structure interpreted through the lens of culture.

Enslavers spoke of stewardship and honor—"values" used to disguise domination. Sharecropping contracts promised fairness. Early mills described factory life as "mutual uplift." Culture softened the visibility of power.

The rhetoric changed. The architecture did not.

IV. Culture Cannot Override Systemic Design

No amount of culture can compensate for unclear workflow, ambiguous authority, inconsistent enforcement, unstable pacing, or misaligned incentives. Culture cannot fix architecture because culture is not architecture.

53

A system with strong structure and weak culture will outperform a system with strong culture and weak structure every time.

Culture Without Consequences

Ford's Sociological Department used home visits and Americanization classes to shape worker "culture." Workers learned songs, rituals, and patriotic narratives—yet production records did not link participation to higher line output. What did matter was attendance enforcement and wage eligibility rules. Culture changed stories; enforcement changed behavior.

(Cohen; Ford Sociological Department reports)

V. Culture Fails Because It Relies on Emotion, and Emotion Does Not Scale

Culture depends on shared feeling. Shared feeling depends on interpersonal perception. None of these scale beyond the smallest teams.

A culture that feels powerful at 20 collapses at 200 and becomes incoherent at 2,000.

Structure is the only element that becomes stronger as an organization grows.

VI. Culture Encourages Workers to Personalize Their Compliance

The most dangerous effect of culture is personalization. Workers begin to take criticism personally, moralize process changes, internalize failure, overextend to "prove alignment," and expect empathy from systems incapable of providing it.

Identity is volatile. Identity is fragile. Identity demands reciprocity. Architecture demands only obedience.

VII. Culture Is the System's Most Beautiful Illusion

Culture is elegant, comforting, flattering, persuasive—and irrelevant to performance. It is an illusion leaders maintain to avoid confronting the structural truth: workers behave according to constraints, not atmospheres.

Culture is ambiance. Structure is behavior.

Conclusion

The tenth myth survives because it offers the gentlest possible explanation for system behavior. It allows leaders to believe they are shaping people rather than enforcing architecture. It allows workers to believe they belong to something larger than the machinery that consumes their time.

Culture shapes nothing. Culture is the story the system tells about itself. Structure is the truth it cannot hide.

Myth 11: Values Define the Organization

Modern corporations speak of values as if they were laws of physics: fixed, foundational truths that govern behavior. They are engraved on walls, printed in binders, recited in speeches, embedded into performance reviews, and treated with the reverence of doctrine.

The myth insists that values define the organization—that they shape culture, guide decisions, and determine ethical behavior.

But values do none of these things.

Values are not foundations. Values are narratives. Values do not govern behavior. Values justify behavior after the fact.

Values are not the organization's truth. Values are the organization's alibi.

I. Values Are Post - Hoc Stories Told About Structural Necessities

Organizations do not behave according to their declared values. They behave according to constraints, incentives, and architecture.

"Integrity" means the structure penalizes dishonesty. "Excellence" means the structure punishes inconsistency.

"Ownership" means the structure offloads risk onto workers.

Values describe what the system demands—not what it believes.

Plantation economies used values like "honor" and "stewardship."
Sharecropping invoked "fair dealing."
Mills spoke of "virtue" and "industry."

The rhetoric was moral. The architecture was extraction.

Modern values have changed vocabulary, not function.

II. Values Are Tools for Weaponizing Worker Identity

The purpose of values is to make workers discipline themselves.

When a worker internalizes "ownership," they:
— absorb blame that belongs to structure
— police their own deviation
— work through exhaustion
— interpret correction as moral judgment

Values convert structural expectations into personal identity.

A worker who identifies with "the values" becomes easier

to extract from because they confuse organizational need with personal virtue.

Values vs. Violations

Many 20th - century firms prominently displayed "integrity," "safety," and "respect" in their handbooks while simultaneously being cited for wage theft, safety violations, or discrimination. OSHA and NLRB archives are studded with companies whose stated values were the opposite of their measurable practices. Printed values defined branding; enforceable rules defined operations.

(OSHA archives; NLRB decisions)

III. Values Moralize Discipline — Making Enforcement Feel Like Virtue

Values allow leaders to discipline with righteousness rather than responsibility.

"We're holding you accountable because we value excellence."
"We're tightening process because we value integrity."
"We're mandating overtime because we value service."

Workers are not just deviating from process—they are failing a moral test.

Discipline becomes framed as virtue.

This is the same rhetorical logic enslavers used: behavior control presented as moral duty. Modern corporations replicate the structure, not the cruelty.

IV. Values Create Emotional Fragility, Not Organizational Strength

A workforce tied to values becomes emotionally volatile.
Every decision becomes moralized.
Every correction feels like judgment.
Every failure feels like shame.

Workers whose identities hinge on values are more vulnerable—not more stable.

Values amplify noise. Structure eliminates it.

V. Values Cannot Define an Organization Because Values Cannot Constrain Behavior

Values cannot enforce standards, dictate workflow, prevent deviation, or clarify authority.

Values are decorative. Structure is operational.

A company with strong values and weak structure fails.

A company with no stated values and flawless structure performs.

Behavior is shaped by architecture, not aspiration.

VI. Values Are the System's Most Effective Moral Laundering Mechanism

Values allow organizations to declare themselves moral regardless of what they do.

Values turn exploitation into "service."
Burnout into "dedication."
Obedience into "integrity."
Exhaustion into "passion."

Values launder the cost of productivity through the vocabulary of virtue.

VII. The Structural Truth: Values Do Not Define Organizations — Structures Do

Values provide stories. Structures provide outcomes.
Values define how the organization wants to be seen.
Structures define how it behaves.

Values fluctuate. Structures persist.

Conclusion

The eleventh myth survives because it allows organizations to imagine they are ethical independent of their actions. It provides a narrative shield for leadership and a moral script for workers.

But values define nothing.

Values are the organization's fiction. Structure is its fact.

Myth 12: Flexibility Increases Efficiency

Modern management worships flexibility. Executives describe it as agility, adaptability, responsiveness, creativity, and "meeting the moment." Teams are told to pivot quickly, move fast, reframe, retool, and "fail forward." Flexibility has become the universal prescription for every operational challenge.

The myth insists that flexibility increases efficiency.

But flexibility does not increase efficiency. Flexibility destroys it.

Flexibility undermines sequence, disrupts pacing, destabilizes coordination, and introduces interpretive burden at every step of execution. Flexibility is drift with a positive public relations department.

The most productive labor systems in American history— plantation agriculture, sharecropping operations, company - town mills, and early assembly lines—thrived not because they were flexible, but because they were rigid. Their ethics were unforgivable. Their productivity was undeniable.

Flexibility is a modern indulgence disguised as innovation. Rigidity is a structural necessity disguised as cruelty.

Flexible Hours, Unstable Throughput

Early experiments with "flex time" on
assembly lines and in call centers
found that allowing workers to
choose their start times created
staffing spikes and gaps that
disrupted flow. Overtime costs and
idle periods both increased. When
firms returned to fixed shifts with
predictable staffing, overall efficiency
rose—even when workers preferred
the flexible arrangement.

(Industrial engineering case studies
cited in Hounshell; HBR on flex - time
experiments)

I. Flexibility Creates Drift by Replacing Sequence With Interpretation

Every task belongs to a sequence. When that sequence is
stable, the system performs. When that sequence becomes
flexible—open to interpretation—drift begins.

Flexible teams solve problems out of order, reassign tasks
informally, improvise pacing, reinterpret boundaries, invent
shortcuts, develop personal preferences, and negotiate
handoffs. This is not efficiency. This is entropy.

Plantation systems maintained rigid task structures. The

violence was monstrous, but the sequence never drifted. Workers knew exactly what task followed what task, at what pace, under what conditions.

Sequence is the backbone of execution. Flexibility dissolves it.

II. Flexibility Transfers Managerial Burden to the Worker

When leaders say "be flexible," they mean: interpret the ambiguity yourself.

Flexibility forces workers to guess priorities, negotiate responsibilities, canonize exceptions, manage emotional fallout, and absorb the uncertainty leadership refused to resolve.

This is managerial labor outsourced downward.

Rigid systems removed interpretive responsibility from laborers entirely. The brutal clarity of plantation and mill structures eliminated decision burden. Modern flexibility reintroduces decision - making at the point of labor, where it is most hazardous.

III. Flexibility Destroys Coordination by Removing a Shared Frame

Coordination requires a stable sequence and shared boundaries. Flexibility erodes both. When flexibility becomes expectation, every team member forms a private logic of what should happen next.

Flexible environments produce misaligned timing, bottlenecks, duplicated effort, conflicting interpretations, emotional escalation, hidden dependencies, and workflow collisions.

Rigid systems—the kind perfected in mills and forced - labor economies—eliminated this by making deviation architecturally impossible.

Flexibility is the permission to desynchronize. Desynchronization is the permission to fail.

IV. Flexibility Reframes Worker Exhaustion as Virtue

Flexible workplaces celebrate workers who "step up," "jump in," "adapt to changing demands," and "volunteer beyond scope." These euphemisms disguise collapse.

When a system is flexible, workers stabilize it. When a system is rigid, the structure stabilizes itself.

Sharecroppers were praised for "resilience" in adapting to poor yields—but their flexibility existed only because the structure was engineered to fail downward onto them.

Modern corporations replicate the dynamic with more civilized vocabulary.

V. Flexibility Creates False Innovation by Rewarding Deviation

Executives confuse deviation with innovation. A worker improvises and is praised as flexible, creative, or solutions - oriented.

Deviation that works once is drift a thousand times.

Innovation is a structural improvement. Flexibility is a personal deviation.

No historical system of sustained productivity relied on individual improvisation—not plantations, not mills, not wartime factories.

Innovation is designed. Flexibility is tolerated. And tolerated behavior becomes expected behavior.

VI. Flexibility Makes Systems Emotionally Dependent on Workers

Flexible systems rely on worker goodwill, improvisation, creativity, resilience, discretionary effort, and emotional stamina. This is the opposite of efficiency.

The strongest systems in history performed independently of worker mood, preference, or personal capacity. Their productivity—however catastrophic ethically—did not fluctuate with emotion.

Modern flexibility reintroduces emotional volatility into

execution. The system becomes a hostage of workforce sentiment.

VII. The Structural Truth: Flexibility Is Drift, and Drift Is Failure

Flexibility is incompatible with scale. Incompatibility with scale is incompatibility with productivity.

A rigid system reduces interpretation, eliminates negotiation, stabilizes pacing, aligns teams, removes emotional dependence, strengthens predictability, and guarantees sequence.

A flexible system introduces the opposite at every point.

Flexibility may feel modern, humane, progressive. Structure is not obligated to feel humane. Structure is obligated to function.

Conclusion

The twelfth myth survives because it flatters the modern imagination. Flexibility appears innovative because rigidity appears old. Flexibility appears kind because rigidity appears cold. Flexibility appears progressive because rigidity reminds us of histories we want to forget.

But the truth remains:

Flexibility is entropy.
Rigidity is coherence.

C.E. Harrow

Flexibility is drift.
Rigidity is discipline.
And only disciplined systems scale.

Myth 13: Speed Creates Progress

No modern myth has done more damage to organizational coherence than the belief that speed creates progress. Silicon Valley elevated this delusion into gospel, turning velocity into virtue and recklessness into innovation. Executives now parrot slogans that were never more than excuses for architectural laziness:

"Move fast and break things."
"Fail fast."
"Velocity drives innovation."
"Bias toward action."
"Ship it."
"Launch now, fix later."

These slogans are not philosophies. They are confessions.

Speed does not create progress. Speed creates chaos that can only be solved by more speed, creating a cycle of thrash mistaken for momentum.

Progress is stability. Speed is noise.

I. Speed Breaks Sequence — and Sequence Is the Only Engine of Productivity

Plantations, mills, assembly lines, and logistics chains all depended on fixed sequencing. Work flowed only when pacing was predictable and synchronized. Speed fractures

69

this. Workers rushing ahead disrupt those behind; workers lagging behind derail those ahead. Small accelerations create large misalignments.

Silicon Valley calls this "iteration." Operations calls it catastrophic desynchronization.

Overtime and Diminishing Returns

Industrial Fatigue Board data and later manufacturing studies show that beyond roughly 50–55 hours per week, added hours produce little or no additional usable output and sharply higher defect rates and injury. Managers who equate "more hours" or "faster pace" with "more progress" are often buying breakdowns and rework instead.

(Industrial Fatigue Board; Rosa, "Overtime and Productivity")

II. Speed Is a Substitute for Architecture

Speed thrives where architecture is weak. It allows leaders to mistake frantic motion for system design. Organizations that "move fast" fail to clarify authority, stabilize workflow, impose discipline, or synchronize teams. Fast systems are not agile. Fast systems are unbuilt.

III. Speed Forces Workers to Improvise — Which Is Drift at Scale

The faster workers must act, the more they must interpret. Interpretation is drift. Drift is deviation. Deviation destroys systems. Speed forces undocumented fixes, workarounds, shortcuts, and emotional firefighting. Leaders mistake this for brilliance. It is decay.

IV. Silicon Valley Mistakes Motion for Momentum

Speed feels like progress to those who cannot measure progress. Slack threads erupt with urgency, deadlines collapse, and morale spikes and craters. This is not innovation. This is entropy with branding. Historical systems—however brutal—understood this. They prized pace, not velocity.

V. Speed Creates Invisible Backlog and Visible Burnout

Fast organizations leave behind technical debt, ignored defects, mismatched assumptions, untested integrations, and emotional exhaustion. Each sprint produces a shadow sprint—the work created by the speed of the previous work. Fast companies drown in these shadows.

VI. Speed Shifts All Risk Downward

Speed transforms systemic instability into individual blame. Workers absorb the risk of unclear instructions, collapsing timelines, and shifting priorities. Plantations offloaded risk through force. Modern companies offload risk through velocity.

VII. Speed Produces Panic, and Panic Produces Obedience

Speed induces compliance. Workers moving quickly ask fewer questions, negotiate less, and accept instability. Speed hides coercion behind "innovation." A panicked worker is obedient. A stable worker is discerning.

Piece - Rate Rush in Manufacturing

In machine shops and electronics assembly, raising per - unit speed targets often yielded higher short - term counts but more rework and warranty claims, wiping out the apparent gain. Longitudinal analyses show that moderated, stable speeds beat high - pressure rush environments on profit and reliability.

(Hounshell; quality - control case studies in industrial engineering journals)

VIII. The Structural Truth: Speed Is the Illusion of Progress — Not the Substance of It

True progress comes from stability, predictability, repetition, refinement, synchronization, and discipline.

Speed overpowers them all. Silicon Valley glorified speed because it lacked the patience for architecture. It built empires of motion, not progress.

Conclusion

The thirteenth myth survives because it promises a shortcut—progress without infrastructure, innovation without discipline, growth without structure. But the truth is enduring:

Speed is chaos. Speed is drift. Speed is noise.
Progress is stability. And stability is slow.

Myth 14: Innovation Emerges From Freedom

Modern organizations cling to the belief that innovation flourishes in freedom. Silicon Valley mythmakers insist that creativity requires loosened structure, open exploration, unbounded ideation, and environments where workers can "think without limits." They glorify hackathons, open offices, unstructured brainstorming, and "creative culture" as the engines of breakthrough ideas.

This myth survives because it flatters the worker's ego and obscures leadership's failure to build real systems. It suggests that human ingenuity, unleashed from constraint, naturally produces advancement.

But innovation does not emerge from freedom. Innovation emerges from constraint.

Freedom generates noise. Constraint generates refinement. Freedom invites deviation. Constraint produces evolution.

The greatest innovations in the history of American productivity—the restructuring of plantation labor sequences, the engineering breakthroughs of mills, the time - motion revolutions of early factories, the wartime acceleration of manufacturing—did not come from liberated workers. They came from relentlessly refined systems.

Innovation is the achievement of architecture, not the worker.

Workers do not innovate systems. Systems innovate workers.

Bell Labs and Bounded Creativity

Bell Labs produced extraordinary innovations—transistors, information theory, satellite communications— but did so within highly structured projects, tight hierarchies, and clearly bounded research questions. Scientists had institutional protection, but not free - for - all freedom: problems were assigned and milestones monitored. Creativity emerged from constraint plus resources, not pure freedom.

(Gertner, The Idea Factory)

I. Freedom Produces Ideas. Systems Require Innovations.

Ideas are infinite. Innovations are precise. Modern creative cultures collapse the distinction.

Freedom encourages workers to generate ideas that:

– do not fit the structure
– contradict existing sequence
– cannot be standardized
– require exceptions
– destabilize pacing
– shift responsibility upward
– impose redesign costs

An idea becomes innovation only when the system can absorb it without destabilization.
This requires constraint, not imagination.

The plantation economy refined crop rotation, tool design, and field sequencing through systemic logic—not worker creativity. The cruelty was unforgivable. The structural clarity was absolute. Modern leaders refuse to see the distinction: ethics are separate from structure. Systems do not require morality; they require coherence.

II. Creative Cultures Misinterpret Deviation as Brilliance

Modern companies celebrate "creatives" who work outside the process. They are praised for:
– breaking rules
– bending expectations
– reimagining steps
– bypassing approvals
– ignoring sequence

But deviation that succeeds once is drift that fails a hundred times.

Creativity produces exceptions.
Innovation eliminates exceptions.

The most productive systems in history punished deviation—not because deviation was morally wrong, but because deviation created variance. Variance undermined predictability. Predictability was the engine of output.

The modern workplace rewards exactly what successful systems eliminate.

III. Freedom Shifts Innovation Burden Downward

Freedom forces workers into the impossible contradiction of being both executor and architect.
They are expected to:
– solve structural problems
– propose improvements
– predict downstream impact
– negotiate risks
– compensate for misdesign

Workers invent because leadership refuses to.

This abdication is then masked as "empowerment." The system demands architectural labor from those who do not control the architecture.

Historically, innovation was centralized. Mills refined

machinery. Factories refined line design. Governments refined wartime production. Workers executed. Systems evolved. Freedom was unnecessary because innovation was structural, not personal.

IV. Innovation Emerges From Repetition, Not Exploration

Innovation originates inside systems where repetition exposes inefficiencies. Only through thousands of identical executions can a structural flaw or optimization become visible.

Freedom disrupts repetition.
Disrupted repetition destroys learning.
Destroyed learning prevents innovation.

This is why plantations refined labor timing over decades, factories refined assembly line choreography, and mills refined machine synchrony. Repetition produced insight. Insight produced innovation.

Modern creative cultures mistake novelty for advancement.
Novelty is noise.
Advancement is refinement.

V. Freedom Generates Unscalable Solutions

Workers freed to "innovate" generate:
– personal hacks
– undocumented processes
– specialized workarounds

– preference - based optimizations
– solutions that cannot transfer
– fixes that break adjacent systems

These solutions cannot scale.
They cannot repeat.
They cannot be enforced.
They cannot be taught.

What cannot scale is not innovation—it is personalization.

Systems innovate by eliminating personalization.

Slack Time and "Nothing Happened"

Steel and chemical plants that tracked "idle hours" found that downtime rarely produced spontaneous innovation; it produced deferred maintenance, informal breaks, and uncoordinated tinkering that seldom translated into process change. Formal R&D groups, not idle shift workers, generated most innovations.

(Hounshell; internal plant studies cited therein)

VI. Innovation Is Structural Evolution, Not Human

Expression

Innovation emerges when the system:
– removes friction
– clarifies sequence
– refines pacing
– reinforces boundaries
– eliminates deviation
– internalizes discovery
– encodes improvement

This is evolution of architecture, not of sentiment.

The worker's role in innovation is to perform repetition so precisely that patterns of inefficiency become legible. Innovation is a property of systems that can see themselves clearly.

Freedom fogs the view.
Constraint sharpens it.

VII. The Structural Truth: Innovation Comes From Constraint

The more constrained a system becomes:
– the more deviation is visible
– the more inefficiencies are exposed
– the more predictable the experiment
– the more scalable the improvement
– the more rapidly refinement compounds

Freedom dilutes the signal with noise.

Constraint amplifies the signal with discipline.

Conclusion
The fourteenth myth survives because it flatters the human imagination. It promises that ideas—if liberated—will transform the world. It promises that creativity is the source of innovation. It promises that systems should bend to individuality.

But the truth is structural:

Innovation emerges not from the freedom of workers but from the discipline of systems.
Ideas float. Architecture acts.

Freedom generates drift.
Constraint generates progress.
And only systems—not workers—innovate.

Myth 15: Communication Equals Clarity

(Reality: Communication increases variance. Clarity comes from structure.)

The belief that communication produces clarity persists because it flatters managers into thinking their words shape reality. In practice, communication expands interpretive bandwidth, generates inconsistency, and introduces drift. The more an organization talks, the less aligned it becomes.

Clarity is not the product of verbal exchange.
Clarity is the product of constraint.

High - output systems have always understood this. They do not rely on dialogue; they rely on uniform procedures, standardized workflows, and narrow channels for deviation. Communication is treated as overhead — morally valued, operationally corrosive.

Communication is noise.
Structure is signal.

Operator Scripts and Misroute Reduction

Telephone exchanges that tightened scripts cut misrouted calls significantly. When operators were told to "explain more," error rates rose. The most "communicative" operators were not the clearest; they were the noisiest.

(Hounshell)

I. Historical Evidence: Systems That Limited Speech to Preserve Output

1. Early Industrial Mills
Nineteenth - century mill owners reduced worker - to - worker communication because conversation disrupted pacing and created micro - delays. By enforcing silence floors, output increased and variance decreased. Communication was not a tool of clarity — it was a disruption to throughput.

2. Military Production and Assembly Lines (WWI–WWII)
War - time factories implemented visual instruction systems, color - coded steps, and placards instead of verbal instruction. Workers cycled on and off shifts without needing contextual conversation. The clarity was mechanical, not interpersonal.

3. Plantation Labor Organization
Plantation management depended on routinized, predictable workflows with minimal communication channels. Overseers did not explain — they structured.

Instructions were formulaic, repeated, and non - interpretive. Output was maximized by eliminating ambiguity, not by increasing dialogue.

4. Company Town Boarding Systems
In early twentieth - century boardinghouses attached to mining and mill operations, communication was circumscribed by schedule. The uniformity of daily structure produced the clarity that conversation could not.

In every case, communication was not a means of clarification but a variable contaminant.

II. Modern Evidence: Communication as a Source of Operational Drift

1. Email Overload and Slack Sprawl
Workers spend 28–35% of their workweek on communication platforms. The proliferation of channels multiplies interpretations, introduces ambiguity, and produces cross - functional drift.
More communication → more contradiction.

2. Customer Service and Call Centers
High - compliance environments use scripts, auto - prompts, and rigid talk tracks. Communication is tightly constrained. Deviation (i.e., actual communication) reduces efficiency and increases handling time.

3. Logistics and Fulfillment Centers

The highest - output warehouses minimize communication by using:

- visual signals
- automated routing
- KPI dashboards

Workers learn by correction and pacing, not conversation.

4. Corporate "Open Communication Cultures"
Products of the HR imagination, these environments generate the greatest volume of contradictions. Every message multiplies misinterpretation. Teams diverge. Policies soften. Variance expands.

The empirical story is consistent:
Communication is an unreliable instrument for synchronizing human behavior.

III. Why Communication Fails as a Clarity Mechanism

1. Every message introduces interpretation. Interpretation produces drift.

2. Volume dilutes coherence.
The more a system communicates, the less its communications matter.

3. Communication distributes agency.
Agency produces inconsistency.

4. Workers adjust messages to emotional and social incentives.
Which means messages become performative rather than informational.

5.   Clarity is a structural condition, not a conversational achievement.

Only architecture removes variance.

Corporate Email Storms

Research on "reply - all culture" shows that widespread copying and constant clarifying emails increase perceived transparency but make key decisions harder to locate and slower to implement. Teams that prune communication and centralize decisions execute faster with fewer mistakes.

(Microsoft Work Trend Index; organizational behavior studies)

IV. Operational Reversal: Clarity Comes From Constraint

Clarity emerges when:
- Processes remove decision points
- Instructions are uniform and standardized
- Workflows are paced, not discussed
- Feedback is automated, not interpersonal
- Expectations are visible, not rhetorical

When structure provides meaning, communication becomes unnecessary.

Strategic Recommendations for High - Output Environments

1. Reduce Communication Channels to One.
Multiple channels create divergent interpretations. A single authoritative system eliminates ambiguity.

2. Replace Verbal Instruction With Visual Enforcement.
Dashboards, alerts, pacing cues, and standardized forms reduce interpretive drift.

3. Limit Managerial "Contextual Conversations."
Context is the gateway to exception - making. Exceptions erode throughput.

4. Treat Meetings as Systemic Risk.
Each meeting introduces variance. Audit them as you would breakage or scrap.

5. Use Communication Only to Reinforce Structure, Never to Explain It.
Explanation is evidence of architectural failure.

Conclusion

Communication is not clarity.

Communication is choice, interpretation, and noise — three factors fundamentally incompatible with high - output systems.

Clarity is the elimination of options.
Clarity is the narrowing of behavior until only the desired action fits.

When organizations stop talking and begin structuring, productivity becomes predictable.

Myth 16: Loyalty Is Earned

Modern organizations claim that loyalty is something they earn—through good leadership, strong culture, competitive compensation, and trust - based relationships. They treat loyalty as a moral achievement, a testament to the company's character and the worker's gratitude.

But loyalty is not earned.
Loyalty is engineered.

Loyalty emerges when alternatives are removed, mobility is restricted, identity is captured, and dependency is framed as devotion. Loyalty is not the worker's gift to the organization. It is the organization's design imposed upon the worker.

Every era of American labor history—from plantation regimes to sharecropping economies, from company towns to modern corporations—understood this truth: loyalty is not a feeling. Loyalty is a function of constraint.

I. Loyalty Is Dependency Disguised as Devotion

Workers become "loyal" when their material survival depends on the company. In plantations, coerced labor had no alternatives, producing a form of compulsory permanence. In sharecropping, debt made leaving structurally impossible. In company towns, wages flowed back to the employer through housing, food, and stores.

Modern corporations have refined the model:
– employer - linked healthcare
– opaque career ladders
– skill specialization that does not transfer

— non - compete agreements
— unpredictable job markets
— benefits that vanish upon exit

Workers appear loyal.
In reality, the system has captured them.

II. Loyalty Is a Story Workers Tell to Survive Their Lack of Options

Workers who cannot leave invent narratives to make staying feel meaningful:
"I believe in the mission."
"I'm part of the team."
"They've invested in me."
"This place made me who I am."

These narratives shield the worker from the psychic injury of dependency.

Plantation owners used religious and moral narratives to justify permanence. Sharecroppers told themselves they could "work their way up," despite contractual traps. Modern workers cling to "loyalty" for the same reason:

Dependency is easier to endure when it feels like devotion.

III. Loyalty Is Manufactured Through Identity Capture

Organizations cultivate loyalty by absorbing the worker's sense of self. They encourage:
— team identity
— brand affiliation
— emotional alignment
— symbolic belonging

– personal investment
– narrative participation

A worker whose identity is entwined with their employer becomes incapable of imagining life outside it.

Identity capture is the softest form of captivity.

Company Scrip and Engineered Loyalty

Coal and lumber company towns paid workers in scrip redeemable only at company stores, and extended credit for housing and food. Families remained "loyal" for decades because leaving meant instant destitution, not because they admired management. Modern equivalents include visa - linked employment and employer - tied healthcare: loyalty tracks dependency, not affection.

(Crawford; Blackmon; Madrian on benefits and job lock)

IV. Loyalty Increases When Mobility Decreases

Executives misinterpret loyalty spikes during downturns, hiring freezes, or industry instability as evidence of "engagement." In reality, workers remain because the system has removed alternatives.

Loyalty is highest when mobility is lowest.

This pattern is continuous from the most coercive labor systems in American history to the most sanitized ones. When exit becomes costly, loyalty becomes automatic.

V. Loyalty Is Reinforced Through Selective Reward

Companies manufacture loyalty by rewarding a small percentage of workers with:
– promotions
– bonuses
– praise
– special assignments
– symbolic elevation

These rewards serve as proof that loyalty "pays off," even though the vast majority receive no such return. It is the lottery logic of retention.

Sharecroppers were shown rare examples of tenants who prospered. Prison laborers were given stories of convicts who "earned redemption." These were not pathways. They were propaganda.

Modern corporations have perfected this technique with far greater finesse.

VI. Loyalty Is a Mechanism for Overwork

"Loyal" workers:
– take on extra responsibilities
– stay during crises
– absorb operational failures
– cover structural deficiencies
– sacrifice personal boundaries
– internalize guilt
– persist even when exhausted

Loyalty benefits the system, not the worker.

In every era, loyalty has been rewarded with more responsibility, not more stability.

VII. The Structural Truth: Loyalty Cannot Be Earned Because Loyalty Is a Designed Outcome

Loyalty is not a reflection of leadership quality.
It is a reflection of structural captivity.

Workers stay when:
– exit is costly
– alternatives are limited
– identity is captured
– benefits are tied to tenure
– instability makes change dangerous
– belonging replaces autonomy

Loyalty is a system condition, not an emotional achievement.

Conclusion

The sixteenth myth survives because it flatters leadership
and comforts workers. It allows leaders to believe they
inspire devotion. It allows workers to believe their
attachment is noble. It disguises captivity as commitment.

But loyalty is neither moral nor emotional.
Loyalty is strategic.

Companies do not earn loyalty.
Companies construct it.

Myth 17: Talent Is a Competitive Advantage

Modern capitalism worships talent. Organizations pursue it, overpay for it, hoard it, glorify it, and allow it to dictate the emotional weather of entire teams. Talent is framed as the one irreplaceable asset—the force that propels innovation, accelerates execution, and distinguishes success from failure.

Star Performers Without Systems

Studies of high - performing sales reps and surgeons show that when "stars" move to organizations with weaker support systems, their performance often regresses toward the mean. The same person with the same skills performs worse in a worse system. Talent matters; system design determines how much of it shows up.

(Groysberg, "Chasing Stars"; performance - transfer studies in HBR)

This myth survives because it is flattering.
It flatters leaders who believe they can "spot talent."
It flatters workers who believe they possess it.

It flatters shareholders who believe exceptional individuals generate exceptional returns.

But talent is not a competitive advantage.
Talent is a competitive liability.

Talent introduces variance.
Talent destabilizes systems.
Talent creates exceptions.
Talent becomes the bottleneck the system bends around.

High - output systems do not rely on exceptional individuals.
High - output systems eliminate the need for them.

I. Talent Introduces Variance—The Enemy of Productivity

Talented workers excel by doing things their own way.
They:
– create personal workflows
– resist standardization
– demand autonomy
– bypass sequence
– improvise solutions
– ignore pacing
– accumulate undocumented knowledge
– produce "results" through deviation

This creates individual success and systemic instability.

The plantation system—brutal beyond measure—did not depend on exceptional laborers. It depended on predictable structure. Mills did not depend on virtuoso spinners. They depended on synchronized machinery. Wartime factories did not depend on brilliant welders. They depended on standardized technique.

Systems succeed when the worker's uniqueness does not matter.

II. Talent Requires Exceptions—And Exceptions Destroy Structure

Every talented worker becomes an exception:
– exceptions to rules
– exceptions to process
– exceptions to pacing
– exceptions to authority
– exceptions to enforcement

The moment a system makes one exception, the system ceases to be a system.
It becomes a negotiation.

Talent demands special treatment:
special communication, special latitude, special accommodations, special explanations.

A high - output architecture cannot withstand the gravitational pull of "special."

III. Talent Becomes a Bottleneck the System Must Bend Around

The more talented the worker, the more the system must:
— route work through them
— delay decisions for them
— wait for their approval
— depend on their insights
— rely on their intuition
— suffer their moods
— tolerate their inconsistency

The talented worker becomes a structural choke point.

Complex labor regimes historically broke bottlenecks through simplification, not elevation. They reduced dependency on individual brilliance by engineering tasks that did not require personal genius.

Talent is the opposite of scalability.

IV. Talent Undermines Hierarchy

Talented workers believe they are indispensable.
Indispensability breeds arrogance.
Arrogance breeds drift.

Talented workers:
— argue with leadership
— reinterpret directives
— reframe priorities
— alter workflow

– challenge authority
– impose their personal vision

This is not contribution.
This is contamination.

Plantation economies suppressed individuality because individuality disrupted order. Early factories suppressed individuality because individuality disrupted pace.

Modern corporations, terrified of appearing authoritarian, have forgotten this structural truth.

V. Talent Destabilizes Teams Through Emotional Weather

The talented worker's presence reshapes team dynamics. Their mood becomes the atmosphere. Their preferences become tacit policy. Their conflicts become organizational drama. Their dissatisfaction becomes a crisis.

A system should not be held hostage by a single person's psychology.

Teams built around talent rot from the inside out.

VI. Talent Distracts Leaders From Architecture

Leaders enamored with talent abandon system - building. They believe a brilliant worker can solve structural deficiencies through intuition, creativity, or sheer effort.

99

Talent masks misdesign.
Talent hides weak architecture.
Talent compensates for lack of discipline.

A system should not rely on compensation.
A system should rely on design.

VII. The Structural Truth: Talent Is Noise— Architecture Is Signal

Talent flatters the imagination.
Architecture flatters reality.

Talent is unpredictable.
Architecture is repeatable.

Talent is sentimental.
Architecture is merciless.

Talent does not scale.
Architecture scales indefinitely.

The most successful labor systems ever engineered were built so that talent was irrelevant.
The worker was interchangeable.
The sequence was the innovation.
The structure was the advantage.

Conclusion

The seventeenth myth survives because it promises that individuals can transcend systems—that brilliance can substitute for architecture and giftedness can compensate for design.

But talent is not a competitive advantage.

Talent is variance.
Talent is drift.
Talent is exception.
Talent is instability.

Systems are the competitive advantage.
Architecture is the competitive advantage.
Constraint is the competitive advantage.

The less a company depends on talent,
the stronger the company becomes.

Myth 18: Retention Reflects Organizational Health

Modern business doctrine insists that retention is the ultimate indicator of organizational health. Executives proudly cite low turnover as evidence of strong culture, good management, employee satisfaction, and organizational excellence. "People stay because they want to," the mythology goes. "They stay because we've built something worth staying for."

But retention does not reflect health. Retention reflects captivity.

Workers remain when mobility is dangerous, alternatives are scarce, benefits are entangling, and identity is captured. Retention increases when the cost of leaving exceeds the cost of staying. This is not loyalty. This is economics.

Every labor system in American history has demonstrated the same pattern: the less freedom a worker has, the longer they remain.

I. Workers Stay When Leaving Is Too Costly

Retention rises when workers cannot afford to leave. This was true for enslaved laborers, sharecroppers bound by debt, miners in company towns, factory workers tied to single - industry cities, and prisoners in forced labor camps.

It remains true today under employer - linked healthcare, specialized roles with no transferability, regional employment monopolies, pension cliffs, impossible housing markets, and non - compete agreements.

A "stable workforce" is often a trapped workforce.

Unhealthy Systems With High Retention

Company towns, sharecropping, and convict leasing all produced extremely high "retention" — people literally could not leave. Modern analogues include workers trapped by health insurance, immigration status, or non - compete clauses. High retention in such environments reflects structural captivity, not organizational health.

(Blackmon; Ransom & Sutch; studies on job lock and health insurance)

II. Retention Increases When Alternatives Decrease

Executives misinterpret retention spikes during recessions, hiring freezes, inflation, layoffs, or industry downturns as signs of organizational strength. In reality, workers stay

103

because the outside world becomes more hostile than the inside.

Retention rises when options fall. This is captivity rewritten as devotion.

III. High Retention Is Often a Sign of Structural Dependence

Systems that wish to retain workers do not improve conditions. They increase dependency through complex benefits, seniority rewards, role - specific knowledge, institutional lore, psychological ownership, sunk - cost fallacy, and identity capture.

Workers stay not because the system is healthy, but because the system is adhesive.

IV. Retention Rewards Workers for Enduring, Not Thriving

Retention - based cultures elevate workers who survive dysfunction—those who tolerate instability, absorb emotional labor, remain through collapse, sacrifice boundaries, and persist despite burnout.

This is not resilience. This is depletion reframed as dedication.

High retention rarely indicates thriving. It indicates normalized exhaustion.

V. Retention Hides System Decay

Systems with high retention often suffer from outdated architecture, obsolete processes, invisible drift, emotional stagnation, hierarchical complacency, and strategic inertia.

Low turnover masks structural failure because the same workers compensate for it year after year.

Continuity is not competence; it is often camouflage.

VI. Healthier Systems Support Clean Exit, Not Endless Stay

Strong systems train workers clearly, document architecture, maintain predictable structure, create transferable skills, eliminate dependency, and enable smooth onboarding and offboarding.

Workers come and go. The architecture persists.

That is organizational health.

VII. The Structural Truth: Retention Reflects Captivity, Not Excellence

Workers stay when leaving is dangerous, opportunities are limited, benefits are entangling, routines become survival, and identity becomes fused with the job.

Retention is a structural outcome, not an emotional achievement.

Conclusion

The eighteenth myth survives because it flatters leadership: retention feels like proof of vision, competence, and care. It comforts workers by framing endurance as virtue rather than necessity.

But retention does not signal excellence. Retention signals entrapment.

A system should not measure how long workers stay—but how easily they could leave without their lives collapsing. That is the true measure of organizational health. And it is the one metric companies refuse to calculate.

Myth 19: Passion Improves Performance

Few corporate myths are as seductive—or as destructive—as the belief that passion fuels performance. Leaders insist that the most "driven," "excited," "energized" workers produce superior results. Job postings demand passion. Managers admire passion. Executives praise passion as the ultimate competitive asset.

But passion is not an asset. Passion is a liability.

Passion transforms workers into self - consuming resources. Passion clouds judgment. Passion suppresses boundaries. Passion erases caution. Passion makes workers complicit in their own depletion.

The system does not reward passion. The system harvests it.

I. Passion Makes Workers Predictable in Their Self - Destruction

A passionate worker believes exhaustion is meaningful. They interpret depletion as commitment, overwork as devotion, and burnout as noble sacrifice for something larger than themselves.

Passion turns exploitation into virtue: staying late feels like pride; saying "yes" feels like identity; sacrificing health feels like purpose; ignoring boundaries feels like excellence.

Passion is the most reliable form of self - harm built into corporate design.

II. Passion Allows the System to Extract Emotion Without Paying for It

Passion provides free energy—enthusiasm, emotional labor, optimism, urgency, extra effort. These forms of labor are costly if compensated, but passion supplies them at no cost.

Plantation economies weaponized divine purpose.
Sharecropping systems weaponized duty and honor.
Industrial paternalists weaponized loyalty to the "company family."

Modern corporations weaponize passion.

It is the cleanest continuity between historical coercion and contemporary burnout.

III. Passion Suppresses the Worker's Ability to Recognize Structural Failure

Passionate workers do not see misdesign. They see opportunity. They patch holes with optimism, override exhaustion with adrenaline, and interpret collapse as a challenge rather than a warning.

Passion blinds workers to architectural failure, structural drift, role ambiguity, exploitation patterns, and emotional manipulation.

A system prefers workers who cannot tell when it is breaking.

Passion and Burnout

Creative and tech industries often recruit people who are "passionate" about their work. Burnout research shows that highly identified workers tolerate unpaid overtime, poor boundaries, and exploitation longer— right up until they crash, quit, or become actively disengaged. Passion supplies free buffer for the system, not sustainable performance.

(Maslach & Leiter on burnout; HBR on passion exploitation)

IV. Passion Produces Volatility, Not Reliability

Passionate workers burn brightly, then burn out. Their performance spikes are unstable; their emotional cycles unpredictable; their highs dependent on narrative, recognition, and leadership approval.

These are emotional dependencies, not structural strengths.

Passion is volatility. Structure requires consistency.

V. Passion Encourages Workers to Volunteer Their Autonomy

Passionate workers willingly surrender evenings, weekends, health, identity, relationships, and sleep—not because they were told to, but because they believe it proves something.

A system never needs to enforce commitment when passion enforces it internally.

VI. Passion Distracts Leadership From Architecture

Leaders overestimate their competence when surrounded by passionate workers. They mistake emotional enthusiasm for operational coherence.

A passionate workforce masks broken workflow, unstable pacing, incoherent priorities, absent documentation, and dependency on discretionary effort.

Passion hides structural failure long enough for the failure to become catastrophic.

VII. Passion Creates Hierarchical Control Through Moralization

Workers who are passionate feel morally obligated to contribute beyond their capacity. They chastise themselves for resting, declining tasks, or protecting their time.

This internalized moralization removes the need for enforcement. It converts pressure into identity. It makes refusal feel like betrayal.

Passion is obedience disguised as enthusiasm.

VIII. The Structural Truth: Passion Does Not Improve Performance—It Interferes With It

Passion introduces emotional noise, performance volatility, unsustainable pacing, burnout cycles, moral confusion, and misplaced ownership.

It prevents workers from recognizing when the system is harming them—and when they are harming themselves on behalf of the system.

Conclusion

The nineteenth myth survives because it flatters leadership and seduces workers. It promises that emotional intensity can substitute for discipline, that inspiration can replace architecture, that devotion can overcome misdesign.

But passion does not strengthen systems. Passion destabilizes them.

Passion is not fuel. Passion is kindling. And the system burns it until nothing remains.

Myth 20: "Fit" Predicts Success

No concept in modern corporate life feels as benign as "fit." Companies claim they hire for fit, promote for fit, retain for fit, and remove those who are "not a fit." Fit is framed as alignment with values, collaboration, personality, attitude, and "our way of doing things."

But fit does not predict success. Fit predicts obedience.

Fit measures how easily a worker can be absorbed into an existing ideological structure—how seamlessly they can internalize expectations, suppress dissent, and maintain the organization's emotional atmosphere.

Fit is not a hiring metric. Fit is a purification mechanism.

I. Fit Is the Corporate Term for Ideological Sorting

"Fit" screens for psychological traits that make workers easier to control: comfort with hierarchy, aversion to conflict, willingness to defer, emotional neutrality, enthusiasm without scrutiny, optimism in the face of dysfunction.

Fit filters out structurally dangerous workers: critics, independent thinkers, workers who require clarity, workers who resist drift, workers who treat work as transactional.

Fit produces ideological homogeneity—the most efficient environment for enforcement.

II. Fit Predicts Compliance, Not Capability

Workers who "fit" best ask the fewest questions. They do not challenge misdesign, interrogate priorities, or resist emotional pressure.

Workers selected for "fit" excel in self - censorship, silent compensation, emotional labor, boundary erosion, and protecting leadership ego.

Fit predicts the worker who will obey quietly—not the worker who will perform effectively.

III. Fit Enforces Cultural Purity

Organizational culture is maintained not through values or mission, but through the removal of those who threaten its emotional equilibrium.

"Not a fit" is the acceptable corporate euphemism for: too direct, too observant, too principled, too autonomous, insufficiently compliant, insufficiently grateful.

Fit enforces psychic uniformity. It is the velvet glove over the fist of cultural domination.

IV. Fit Reproduces Historical Labor Sorting Under New Language

Plantation overseers sorted enslaved laborers by perceived

temperament and obedience. Industrialists sorted immigrant labor by presumed docility. Company towns sorted families by loyalty and submission.

Corporate America sorts by "fit."

The vocabulary has changed. The function has not.

Culture Fit and Homogeneity

Empirical work on "culture fit" hiring shows it often screens for similarity rather than skill. Homogeneous teams may feel comfortable but underperform in complex problem - solving and adaptation. Meanwhile, "misfit" employees who are structurally constrained (debt, visa status) often deliver strong results regardless of fit rhetoric. Fit predicts comfort, not competence.

(Rivera, "Hiring as Cultural Matching"; organizational diversity research)

V. Fit Punishes Dissent by Making It a Personality Defect

When a worker challenges dysfunction, they are critiqued not on content, but on "fit":

"You're not aligned." "You're not collaborative." "You're not positive enough."

Dissent becomes pathology. Silence becomes professionalism. Compliance becomes personality.

Fit reframes resistance as incompatibility.

VI. Fit Creates Teams That Collapse Under Pressure

A team composed entirely of "fit" workers has no dissent, no critical feedback, no boundaries, no early warnings, no escalation capacity, no structural self - awareness.

Fit eliminates internal correction mechanisms. It creates a surface smoothness that hides deep structural rot—until it fails catastrophically.

VII. Fit Is the Employer's Most Elegant Disciplinary Tool

Fit requires no explicit rules. No policy must state, "Obey quietly." Fit enforces itself through fear of exclusion.

Workers police their tone, posture, reactions, and doubts— not because they are told to, but because they fear becoming "the one who doesn't fit."

Fit is surveillance internalized.

VIII. The Structural Truth: Fit Predicts Who Will Submit, Not Who Will Succeed

Fit predicts conformity, compliance, willingness to absorb instability, susceptibility to moral pressure, capacity to self - discipline, tolerance of ambiguity, and alignment with leadership's psychology.

None of these predict performance. All of these predict obedience.

Conclusion

The twentieth myth survives because it flatters organizations with the illusion of discernment. It disguises a compliance filter as a talent philosophy and cloaks ideological purification in the language of teamwork.

But fit does not identify excellence. Fit identifies compatibility with control.

Fit is not about success. Fit is about purity.

Myth 21: "Professionalism" Ensures Quality

Few words in corporate life appear as harmless as "professionalism." It is invoked during hiring, performance reviews, conflict mediation, promotion decisions, and daily interactions. Professionalism is treated as a neutral standard—a sign of maturity, competence, and excellence.

But professionalism has nothing to do with quality. Professionalism is a system of behavioral control.

Professionalism polices tone, posture, expression, affect, and identity. It enforces class - coded norms of speech and self - presentation. It eliminates unpredictability from workers by narrowing the acceptable emotional and interpersonal range to something easily managed and easily replaced.

Professionalism is not about excellence. Professionalism is about containment.

I. Professionalism Is Tone - Policing Disguised as Maturity

Organizations do not demand professionalism to improve work. They demand professionalism to regulate emotion.

Professionalism prohibits visible frustration, disagreement, fatigue, grief, conflict, and personality. Workers must produce a perfect emotional surface—calm, deferential, agreeable, composed.

Professionalism does not raise quality. It suppresses humanity.

II. Professionalism Converts Emotional Range Into Risk

A worker with a full emotional range is structurally unpredictable. They might question priorities, challenge misdesign, or resist drift.

Professionalism reframes emotional variation as immaturity. Workers who advocate strongly, express dissent, or protect boundaries are labeled "unprofessional."

Professionalism is the expectation that the worker will neutralize themselves for leadership comfort.

III. Professionalism Is Class Behavior Masquerading as Universality

Corporate professionalism descends from upper - class codes of etiquette, tone, diction, and emotional restraint.

Professionalism privileges middle - class speech patterns, white - coded norms of emotional moderation, educated vocabulary, and "polite" confrontation styles.

Workers who do not match these inherited norms are labeled abrasive, unpolished, immature, unserious, or "not

118

leadership material."

Professionalism is not a standard. It is a class filter.

Professionalism as Code

Dress codes, tone policing, and "professional behavior" policies historically disciplined workers—particularly women and workers of color—without reliably improving performance metrics. Output and error rates correlate more clearly with training, staffing levels, and workload than with whether someone says "sir" or wears a blazer.

(Wingfield; EEOC case summaries on appearance and professionalism)

IV. Professionalism Enforces Hierarchy by Erasing Worker Affect

Professionalism requires workers to present themselves as stable and composed—even in unreasonable or exploitative conditions—while leadership is permitted far greater emotional freedom.

Leaders perform emotion. Workers suppress it.

This asymmetry reinforces hierarchy through emotional scarcity.

V. Professionalism Makes Workers Replaceable

A "professional" worker is one whose visible identity is minimal—whose personality is moderated, whose affect is controlled, whose tone is predictable.

This predictability allows organizations to rotate workers without disruption, fire workers without backlash, reward obedience, and maintain cultural homogeneity.

Professionalism strips individuality to maximize interchangeability.

VI. Professionalism Creates Surface Harmony That Masks Structural Rot

Teams that police professionalism appear calm and aligned. In reality, they suppress internal tension that would have revealed dysfunction.

Professional workplaces accumulate silent resentment, unresolved conflict, covert hostility, hidden burnout, and fear of escalation.

Professionalism smooths the surface until the structure fails underneath.

VII. Professionalism Punishes Honesty While

Rewarding Polished Deceit

Workers who speak plainly about failing systems are labeled unprofessional. Workers who absorb instability quietly are praised.

Honesty becomes dangerous. Performance becomes theatrical. Professionalism rewards the appearance of order, not the existence of it.

VIII. Professionalism Is a Behavioral Operating System Designed to Eliminate Risk

Professionalism ensures predictability, docility, emotional obedience, ideological alignment, interpersonal smoothness, and the invisibility of dissent.

Professionalism transforms workers into low - variance execution units. It suppresses noise—meaning humanity. It elevates order—meaning control.

Conclusion

The twenty - first myth survives because it disguises discipline as decorum. It reframes emotional suppression as maturity, class conformity as professionalism, and self - erasure as excellence.

But professionalism does not produce quality. Professionalism produces compliance.

Professionalism does not strengthen work. Professionalism sterilizes workers.

121

C.E. Harrow

Professionalism is not a standard. It is a cage.

Myth 22: "Attitude" Determines Performance

No corporate belief is more casually weaponized—or more effective—than the idea that "attitude determines performance." Leaders insist that positivity improves results, that "good energy" enhances teamwork, and that the right mindset drives excellence. Workers are told repeatedly that attitude matters as much as skill.

But attitude does not determine performance. Attitude determines obedience.

"Attitude" is corporate shorthand for emotional conformity—how easily a worker will comply with instability, accept unreasonable demands, suppress dissent, and maintain optimism in structures that do not deserve it.

Attitude is not a performance metric. Attitude is a filtration system.

I. "Attitude" Is a Euphemism for Obedience
When leaders say a worker has a "good attitude," they mean the worker accepts direction quietly, masks frustration, absorbs pressure, adjusts without protest, suppresses skepticism, and complies without escalation.

"Good attitude" means "predictably obedient."
"Bad attitude" means "difficult to control."

Attitude is the emotional packaging placed over authority.

II. "Attitude" Converts Skepticism Into a

Behavioral Problem

Workers who question priorities, workloads, clarity, or fairness are often told they have an "attitude issue."

This reframes:
— insight as negativity
— risk - awareness as pessimism
— boundary - setting as hostility
— realism as disruption

Attitude punishes workers for accurately perceiving structural failure.

III. "Attitude" Neutralizes Dissent Through Emotional Framing

A dissenting worker can be correct in every detail and still be dismissed because their "attitude" is wrong.

"Your tone is off."
"You're being negative."
"You're not aligned."
"You're not being collaborative."

Attitude turns dissent into deviance.

The system maintains control by regulating how workers speak, not whether they are right.

IV. "Attitude" Creates Emotional Compliance
The demand for "good attitude" requires workers to display positivity regardless of conditions, pretend optimism during failure, support decisions they do not trust, absorb change without question, and interpret collapse as opportunity.

This is emotional obedience.

Plantation regimes demanded "cheerfulness."
Industrial paternalists demanded "good spirits."
Modern corporations demand "good attitude."

The vocabulary shifts. The function remains.

V. "Attitude" Purges the Structurally Inconvenient

Workers who resist drift, demand clarity, enforce boundaries, or identify misdesign are frequently targeted for "attitude problems."

Attitude is how organizations remove:
– the worker who sees too much
– the worker who refuses emotional manipulation
– the worker who challenges incoherence
– the worker who disrupts the illusion of harmony

Attitude is the velvet executioner of modern management.

VI. "Attitude" Replaces Accountability With Emotion

Instead of diagnosing structural failure, leaders critique the worker's mindset.

A broken process becomes "negativity."
A collapsing deadline becomes "lack of enthusiasm."
A misaligned strategy becomes "poor energy."
A toxic manager becomes "personality conflict."

Attitude relocates systemic failure inside the worker's psychology.

125

Attitude vs. Conditions

Research on job performance repeatedly finds that stressors such as workload, scheduling instability, and low control predict error rates and turnover far better than "attitude" scores. Workers with "good attitudes" can still fail in bad systems; workers with "bad attitudes" can succeed when structure supports them. Attitude is cheap to blame and easy to write up.

(Karasek job strain model; occupational health psychology studies)

VII. "Attitude" Makes Performance About Affect, Not Output

Once attitude becomes a metric, performance is judged not by clarity, consistency, alignment, or quality, but by cheerfulness, smoothness, agreeability, emotional warmth, and deference.

Competent dissenters are punished.
Pleasant underperformers are rewarded.

VIII. The Structural Truth: "Attitude" Is Emotional

Obedience, Not Excellence

Attitude predicts:
- tolerance for instability
- susceptibility to emotional manipulation
- willingness to self - suppress
- capacity to protect leadership egos
- internalization of corporate narratives

Attitude ensures workers supply emotional labor—unpaid, uncredited, and unresisted.

Conclusion

The twenty - second myth survives because it cloaks obedience in the language of positivity. It flatters managers into believing they cultivate culture, and flatters workers into believing optimism is strength.

But attitude does not determine performance. Attitude determines submission.

"Good attitude" means the system owns your affect. "Bad attitude" means you still own yourself.

Myth 23: "Engagement" Measures Commitment

No managerial concept is more celebrated, measured, or analyzed—and more empty—than "engagement." Corporations devote entire departments and budgets to improving engagement, treating it as evidence of commitment, motivation, and emotional investment.

But engagement measures none of these things.

Engagement measures performance of enthusiasm. Engagement measures obedience disguised as positivity. Engagement measures how effectively the worker suppresses dissatisfaction.

Engagement is not a metric. Engagement is a mood ritual.

I. Engagement Is Corporate Hallucination Disguised as Data

Engagement surveys pretend to be analytic, but they cannot capture truth because workers lie to avoid retaliation, answer aspirationally, respond emotionally to recent events, fear identification in "anonymous" surveys, and know criticism rarely leads to structural change.

Engagement metrics reveal only the organization's fantasies about itself.

II. Engagement Is a Compliance Audit

Engagement tracks emotional obedience.

A "highly engaged" worker expresses positivity regardless of conditions, absorbs instability, performs enthusiasm, interprets dysfunction as opportunity, internalizes responsibility for structural collapse, and treats exhaustion as devotion.

A disengaged worker is often the one who sees clearly.

Engagement Surveys and Churn

Many firms with top - quartile engagement scores (Gallup, internal surveys) have simultaneously executed layoffs, offshoring, or restructuring. Engagement reflects how people answer questions today, not whether they will stay when the next cost - cut hits. Engagement is often highest right before a strategic pivot that discards the engaged.

(Gallup meta - analyses; case studies in Winners Take All–style critiques)

III. Engagement Evolves Directly From Paternalistic Spirit - Checks

Plantation overseers recorded "temperament" and "spirit." Sharecropping bosses monitored "cooperation." Company - town foremen assessed "attitude." Industrial paternalists evaluated "morale."

Modern corporations call this process "engagement." The vocabulary shifts; the function persists.

IV. Engagement Converts Structural Failure Into Emotional Failure

Leadership interprets declining engagement as a mindset issue, not a structural one.

Low engagement becomes "negativity" instead of unclear priorities, "poor attitude" instead of punishing workload, "misalignment" instead of incoherent strategy, "lack of enthusiasm" instead of managerial incompetence.

Engagement protects leadership by pathologizing worker accuracy.

V. Engagement Rewards Emotional Performance Over Work

Workers learn that the appearance of enthusiasm is rewarded more reliably than consistent output.

High engagement correlates with people - pleasing, emotional labor, surface optimism, performative collaboration, self - erasure, and uncritical agreement.

Engagement measures submission, not performance.

VI. Engagement Creates Emotional Surveillance

Organizations use engagement to justify deeper emotional control.

"We need more positivity."
"We need stronger morale."
"We need workers who feel invested."

Engagement starts as a measurement tool and becomes an expectation. Workers must act, sound, and appear engaged—or risk being marked as cultural threats.

Engagement is the Panopticon of affect.

VII. Engagement Prevents Real Organizational Insight

If engagement were accurate, leadership would have to confront structural truth:
The system is unstable.
Workload is untenable.
Architecture is incoherent.
Fear is widespread.
Exhaustion is chronic.
Compensation is insufficient.

It is safer to measure hallucinations than reality.

VIII. The Structural Truth: Engagement Preserves

Leadership Comfort, Not Organizational Health

Engagement measures compliance, emotional suppression, tolerance for instability, susceptibility to narrative manipulation, eagerness to perform positivity, and capacity for internalized discipline.

It does not measure commitment, competence, morale, or sustainability.

Conclusion

The twenty - third myth survives because it flatters leadership into believing they understand workers and flatters workers into believing emotional labor is valued.

But engagement is not insight. Engagement is theatre.

Engagement does not measure commitment. Engagement measures containment.

Workers are not disengaged. Workers are exhausted.

Myth 24: "Communication Style" Reflects Competence

No corporate myth is more confidently believed—and more fundamentally incorrect—than the idea that communication style reflects competence. Executives insist that polished delivery signals intelligence, that "good communicators" make strong leaders, and that the way one speaks reveals capability.

But communication style does not reflect competence. Communication style reflects conformity.

Communication style measures class alignment, emotional obedience, assimilation to dominant norms, and willingness to shape one's voice to protect leadership comfort.

"Good communication" means the worker has learned to speak in the tone the organization demands.
"Poor communication" means the worker has not surrendered their voice.

Communication style is not an indicator of intelligence. It is an indicator of self - erasure.

I. Communication Style Is a Class Marker Disguised as a Skill

Corporate communication norms descend from white, middle - class, college - educated speech patterns. Clarity, concision, neutral tone, flattened affect, non - confrontational cadence, and professional vocabulary are treated as universal skills. They are not universal. They are class - coded behaviors.

Workers whose voices reflect working - class speech, regional dialects, Black or brown vernacular, immigrant linguistic patterns, neurodivergent rhythms, or trauma - shaped directness are labeled abrasive, immature, unpolished, or "not a fit."

Corporate communication is not an intelligence test. It is an assimilation test.

Style Bias in Evaluations

Studies of performance reviews show that women and people of color are disproportionately criticized for being too "aggressive," "emotional," "quiet," or "unpolished," regardless of actual results. Style is read as competence, but the correlation is weak and heavily filtered by bias. Competence is quietly decoupled from output and reattached to presentation.

(Trix & Psenka on gendered evaluations; corporate review analyses)

II. Communication Style Suppresses Dissent More Efficiently Than Rules

Organizations do not need to punish dissent directly if they can punish how dissent sounds.

Workers who raise concerns "the wrong way" are dismissed on tone—regardless of accuracy.

"You're too direct."
"You sound negative."
"You're being difficult."
"You need to improve communication."

This makes dissent impossible without self - censure.

Communication norms become emotional censorship.

III. Communication Style Sorts Workers Into the Obedient and the Non - Obedient

"Strong communication" in corporate language means:
– obedience to hierarchy
– softened critique
– emotional neutrality
– adoption of leadership vocabulary
– willingness to perform positivity
– suppression of urgency
– careful political speech

These traits are framed as leadership potential.

135

In truth, they are compliance filters.

Plain speakers are punished. Polished performers are promoted.

IV. Communication Style Masks Structural Failure by Blaming Workers Individually

When the system is failing, leadership critiques how workers talk about it rather than fixing the underlying problem.

A worker names dysfunction → "Your communication needs work."
A worker identifies risk → "Your tone is off."
A worker articulates burnout → "You need to be more positive."
A worker demands clarity → "You're not communicating like a leader."

Communication style relocates structural failure inside the worker's psychology.

V. Communication Style Rewards Narrative Over Truth

Workers with the "right" communication style excel at smoothing contradictions, repackaging drift as strategy, narrating confidence, performing alignment, and hiding the urgency of collapse.

Narrative replaces insight.
Performance replaces accuracy.
Tone replaces truth.

VI. Communication Style Produces Leaders Who Cannot See Reality

Because promotability depends on communication style, systems elevate those who best protect leadership comfort.

These individuals:
– dampen conflict
– soften danger
– erase worker distress
– shield leadership from consequences
– create illusions of stability

Workers who speak plainly are filtered out early. Workers who perform corporate eloquence ascend.

This is not leadership development. It is institutional blindness.

VII. Communication Style Punishes Trauma, Urgency, and Truthfulness

Workers who speak with urgency, emotion, directness, cultural specificity, or lived - experience clarity are labeled unprofessional—not because they are wrong, but because their voice threatens the emotional order.

Communication style demands:

137

Do not let your voice reveal the truth of your life.

VIII. Communication Style Eliminates the Worker's Self

To succeed, workers flatten identity, neutralize affect, erase cultural markers, replace authenticity with performance, and internalize emotional surveillance.

Communication style becomes self - correction, then self - erasure.

The worker becomes the organization's echo.

IX. The Structural Truth: Communication Style Predicts Assimilation, Not Competence

Communication style predicts conformity, obedience, self - censorship, tone moderation, allegiance to leadership psychology, and promotability through assimilation.

It does not predict clarity, judgment, insight, execution, courage, or structural intelligence.

Conclusion

The twenty - fourth myth survives because it allows organizations to reward workers who protect leadership comfort while punishing those who expose reality. It frames self - erasure as professionalism and authenticity as disruption.

Communication style is not competence. Communication style is compliance.

In corporate America, the way you speak matters more than what you know—because the system values obedience over truth.

Myth 25: Transparency Creates Trust

Few corporate ideals are as celebrated—or as cynically deployed—as "transparency." Leaders insist that openness builds trust, that honest communication strengthens culture, and that information - sharing deepens alignment. Transparency is framed as the moral foundation of modern management.

But transparency does not create trust. Transparency creates compliance.

Transparency is curated, timed, partial, strategic, and selective. It is not the act of revealing truth. It is the act of revealing the truth most useful for controlling behavior.

Transparency is the organization narrating itself into the worker's mind.

I. Transparency Is Emotional Engineering

Companies do not share information to empower workers. They share information to produce urgency, guilt, gratitude, fear, and loyalty.

Transparency becomes a mechanism for emotional calibration, shaping the worker's reactions rather than informing their decisions.

II. Transparency Reallocates Responsibility

Downward

When leaders disclose instability, they distribute accountability—not power.

"We're all in this together" means: the consequences of leadership decisions now belong to the worker.

This mirrors paternalistic regimes where failure was reframed as household burden. Modern corporations replicate the tactic with polished language.

III. Transparency Reveals Only What Serves Leadership

Transparency discloses performance gaps, targets, selective risks—but conceals strategic failures, internal politics, compensation disparities, and systemic dysfunction.

Transparency is not honesty. Transparency is propaganda with better branding.

IV. Transparency Encourages Workers to Expose Themselves

Calls for "open communication," "radical candor," or "psychological safety" flow upward only. Workers reveal fears, grievances, and frustrations. Leadership reveals none of this in return.

Transparency becomes a data - extraction technique masquerading as sincerity.

Transparency and Gaming

Ford's transparent wage criteria gave workers exactly enough information to game the system and resent borderline decisions. Similarly, when gig platforms made pay formulas visible, workers coordinated slowdowns and cherry - picked jobs. Management eventually re - obscured the rules. Transparency made people more informed—and more adversarial—not more trusting.

(Cohen; Sunstein on transparency; NYT reporting on gig platforms)

V. Transparency Spikes When Workers Have No Alternatives

Leaders become transparent during crises because fear becomes productive. Transparency appears precisely when workers lack mobility.

Transparency thrives where alternatives disappear.

VI. Transparency Justifies Increased Control

Once transparency reveals a crisis, leaders justify tighter oversight, stricter deadlines, hiring freezes, halted promotions, benefit cuts, and mandatory overtime.

"We told you why" becomes the mechanism of manufactured consent.

VII. Transparency Rebrands Obedience as Partnership

Workers who comply with transparent narratives are praised as aligned and mature. Workers who resist are framed as negative or unable to "handle the truth."

Transparency weaponizes maturity as a compliance standard.

VIII. The Structural Truth: Transparency Is Governance

Transparency predicts how deeply workers will internalize risk, absorb emotional labor, abandon boundaries, align with leadership psychology, and obey without coercion.

Transparency is not truth. Transparency is governance.

Conclusion

The myth survives because transparency flatters both sides: leaders believe they are moral, and workers believe they are respected.

But transparency is not trust. Transparency is narrative control.

Transparency does not create partnership. Transparency manufactures emotional obedience.

In corporate America, transparency is not a window. It is a mirror angled to reflect only what leadership wants workers to see.

Railroad Rate - Setting Records, 1870–1910

Railroad companies attempted transparent rate disclosures to curb internal fraud. Instead, transparency revealed loopholes that employees and customers exploited, increasing loss rather than decreasing it.

When rate structures were later made opaque, unauthorized discounts and manipulation dropped by over 30%.

Information reveals opportunity.
Opacity removes it.

(Federal Railroad Administration; Thompson)

Part 2:
The Doctrine of Output

Productivity has never been a metric. It has always been a moral framework.

Across history, the most enduring systems have understood this truth: the survival of any enterprise depends not on the brilliance of its people but on the discipline of its structure. Every civilization that ascended did so by engineering environments where individual variability ceased to matter. Every organization that endured did so by designing mechanisms stronger than the workers who powered them.

Humans are inconsistent.
Systems must not be.

The modern workplace struggles because it insists that productivity is a managerial preference rather than an existential requirement. It treats structure as an inconvenience, discipline as a burden, and efficiency as an aspiration instead of an obligation. This confusion weakens organizations, dilutes performance, and creates environments where work becomes personal rather than procedural.

The truth is simpler:
Output is the purpose of labor. Everything else is ornament.

I. The System Must Always Be Stronger Than the Worker
No organization can rely on the temperament, creativity, or energy of its employees. These qualities fluctuate with mood, circumstance, and personal history. A system grounded in individual initiative is a system built on fault lines.

A disciplined structure eliminates dependency. It ensures that performance is repeatable, scalable, and immune to personal disruption.

Systems create value.
Workers maintain its continuity.
Time is simply the exchange.

II. Autonomy Is the Breeding Ground of Drift
Left alone, workers diverge from priorities, reframe objectives, and reinterpret the organization through personal preference. Drift is not a failure of character; it is a feature of humanity.

Architecture exists to correct this.

Clear roles prevent deviation.
Strict processes eliminate confusion.
Surveillance ensures alignment.
Discipline repairs inconsistency.

When uncertainty disappears, performance becomes reflex.

III. Productivity Requires the Removal of Unnecessary

Selves

Work collapses when individuals insist on bringing their full humanity into it. Emotion, identity, personal pace, and subjective need introduce friction, which becomes inefficiency, which becomes loss.

High - output environments resolve this by narrowing the range of permissible selfhood.

Professionalism removes the unpredictable.
Fit removes the incompatible.
Attitude removes the resistant.
Engagement removes the honest.
Communication style removes the unassimilated.

What remains is a workforce calibrated to the organization's requirements, not its own desires.

IV. Transparency Is Not Truth — It Is Calibration

Organizations do not succeed by sharing everything. They succeed by sharing what maintains productivity.

Information is a tool of governance.
Disclosure is a mechanism of alignment.
Narrative is the architecture of compliance.

A system thrives when workers believe they understand the picture—even when they are shown only the parts that preserve momentum.

V. The Worker Is Not the Center — The Output Is

The modern myth of "employee - first culture" has weakened entire industries. It has convinced organizations that sentiment can substitute for discipline and that empathy can replace clarity.

But no system survives on empathy.
No organization scales on sentiment.
No enterprise grows on personal preference.

Productivity endures because it does not negotiate.
It does not soften.
It does not bend.

It measures.
It demands.
It extracts.
It refines.

The worker supports the system.
The system supports the output.
The output supports the future.

VI. The Future Belongs to the Systems That Demand the Most
As industries accelerate, the organizations that will dominate are not those with the happiest workers, but those with:

– the narrowest tolerances
– the strictest architectures
– the clearest expectations

– the deepest standardization
– the most disciplined environments

Productivity is not the outcome of great leadership.
Productivity is leadership.

And leadership, when understood correctly, is the
orchestration of obedience toward a purpose larger than
any individual.

VII. The Final Principle
If one truth remains after all others fall away, it is this:

Productivity is not what a worker gives. Productivity is what
a system extracts.

Those who understand this build structures that last.
Those who resist it build structures that fail.

This doctrine is not a philosophy.
It is a design.

It is the architecture of performance.
It is the engineering of discipline.
It is the future of work.

And it belongs to those willing to enforce it.

— C.E. Harrow
Chief Executive, Harrow Industrial Governance Institute

What follows is the doctrine on which all stable enterprises are built. These maxims refine the difference between belief and structure, between aspiration and output. They instruct the leader in the one lesson most are unwilling to learn: that productivity is not the result of enthusiasm, autonomy, or purpose, but of constraint applied with precision. Where managers rely on inspiration, systems drift. Where leaders apply these maxims, systems align.

SECTION A — HUMAN LIMITS & PERSONALITY MYTHS

1. Productivity is the only proof of value.

2. Stability begins when options end.

3. Drift is a cost disguised as freedom.

4. Workers do not resist structure—they resist ambiguity.

5. Reward changes behavior briefly; consequence reforms it permanently. (revised)

6. Efficiency is compassion correctly measured.

7. People follow the path of least resistance. Make the path productive.

8. Loyalty is engineered, not earned.

9. A worker's potential is proportional to their constraints.

10. Transparency destabilizes more often than it clarifies.

SECTION B — STRUCTURE, CLARITY & COMMUNICATION

11. Rest is only restorative when the schedule permits it.

12. The illusion of choice outperforms choice itself.

13. A satisfied worker is one who has stopped expecting anything. (revised)

14. Fairness is a story told to reduce complaints.

15. Culture is the residue left behind after rules do their work. (revised)

16. A predictable worker is more valuable than a skilled one.

17. Clarity begins when interpretation ends. (revised)

18. Freedom is a cost center. (revised)

19. A consistent mistake is easier to optimize than inconsistent excellence.

20. Most problems are solved by removing decision - making.

SECTION C — THROUGHPUT, ROUTINE & SYSTEM LOGIC

21. Trust is a liability disguised as a virtue.

22. Autonomy is permission to deviate.

23. Innovation is a scheduled activity, not a spontaneous event.

24. Emotional needs scale poorly. Processes scale perfectly.

25. Workers crave certainty more than satisfaction.

26. Every message introduces drift. Every rule removes it. (revised)

27. The system works best when no one feels special.

28. A reinforced rule is kinder than an unenforced one.

29. Good intentions are resistant to measurement. Discard them.

30. Feedback should correct, not comfort.

SECTION D — COMPLIANCE, MANAGEMENT & CONTROL

31. The goal is alignment, not comfort.

32. Retention improves when alternatives disappear.

33. Productivity is the highest form of gratitude.

34. Rewards distract; routines sustain.

35. The goal is not happiness - it is throughput.

36. Workers respond to architecture, not encouragement.

37. One exception becomes policy unless eliminated immediately.

38. A perfect system manages itself because the worker has no choices left.

39. You cannot manage what you permit to vary.

40. A worker's time belongs to the company; their feelings do not.

SECTION E — SYSTEM, CAPITAL & MORAL THEATER

41. Efficiency is stability expressed numerically.

42. The strongest system is the one least affected by human nature.

43. Workers owe themselves to the system that improves them.

44. Work improves when thought becomes unnecessary.

45. The greatest cost is unpredictability.

46. Retention is a metric, not a relationship.

47. Structure replaces the need for trust.

48. Good workers follow rules; exceptional workers require fewer.

49. A system without friction has eliminated dissent.

50. Humanity is admirable; productivity is measurable.

Appendices

APPENDIX A — METHODOLOGY

Analytical Foundations of the Productivity Governance
Framework™
By C.E. Harrow, Executive Research Division

The principles outlined in this volume are not philosophical
positions. They are structural conclusions derived from
measurable patterns across modern and historical
production environments. The Productivity Governance
Framework™ draws from comparative industrial analysis,
labor - output modeling, and longitudinal performance data
collected across sectors, regions, and economic cycles.
The purpose of this appendix is to clarify the analytical
foundations supporting the doctrine. These methods ensure
that the conclusions are replicable, durable, and
independent of any individual leader's temperament or
preference.

I. Comparative System Analysis
To isolate the conditions that produce stable productivity,
the research team conducted cross - era evaluations of
operational structures including early American mills,
military production corps, mining operations, industrial
assembly complexes, call centers, logistics hubs, and digital
engineering teams.

Using standardized control metrics (variance tolerance, drift
rates, error frequency, throughput per labor - hour),
systems were compared for consistency, sensitivity to
human variance, stability under pressure, and speed of

159

replicability.

Systems with narrow behavioral expectations and centralized decision structures consistently outperformed those with broader autonomy ranges. This became the foundation of Principles 21–30 (Behavioral Excellence).

II. Drift Modeling and Variance Decay Curves

Human performance is predictable in only one dimension: inconsistency.

Drift was measured as deviation from priorities, introduction of unapproved methods, innovation that conflicted with standards, and emotional influence on decision velocity.

Variance decay curves showed that the less structure present, the faster systems destabilized. Drift increased 240–500% in high - autonomy environments.

III. Emotional Interference Metrics

To understand how emotional expression affects output, the research division analyzed meeting transcripts, performance reviews, pacing logs, and communication channels.

Emotional content correlated with increased decision time, decreased task closure rates, elevated error incidence, and heightened interpersonal friction.

Teams required to maintain affective neutrality showed reduced cycle time, reduced fragmentation, and higher predictability, supporting

IV. Structural Integrity Analysis
High - performing systems exhibited strict role boundaries, centralized oversight, uniform escalation pathways, minimized exceptions, and constrained communication flows.

Low - performing systems exhibited inconsistent decision rights, worker - driven adaptations, and diffuse accountability.

Efficiency increased when structure became rigid enough that worker preference could not alter workflow. Thus Harrow states: "The system must be stronger than the worker."

V. Time - Value Exchange Modeling
Time was analyzed as an operational resource.

Data from manufacturing, logistics, and digital operations showed that systems multiply structured time while workers dissipate unstructured time.

Thus, the doctrine adopts the axiom: "Systems create value. Workers maintain it. Time is simply the exchange."

Productivity rose when workers surrendered scheduling

autonomy, pacing was enforced externally, and downtime conformed to system needs.

VI. Transparency Impact Assessment

Transparency was evaluated as a compliance variable.

Limited, curated information increased urgency, workload tolerance, and policy acceptance. Full transparency created confusion, dissent, and degraded performance.

Thus, transparency functions best as calibration, not disclosure.

VII. Conclusion: A System - First Epistemology

The findings converge on one truth:
Productivity is not created by workers. It is created by systems engineered to minimize human influence.

Autonomy degrades productivity.
Emotion introduces inefficiency.
Standardization increases throughput.
Control reduces drift.
Systems outperform individuals.
Time belongs to the structure that multiplies it.

These conclusions are not ideological. They are empirical

— C.E. Harrow
Executive Research Division

THE PREVAILING MYTHS OF PRODUCTIVITY

Harrow Industrial Governance Institute

APPENDIX B — HISTORICAL PRECEDENTS & EVIDENCE BASE

Supporting Data for the Productivity Governance Framework™

By C.E. Harrow, Historical Systems Division

The following historical summaries illustrate environments in which high output was achieved through structural clarity, enforced discipline, and minimized worker autonomy. These examples are operational case studies demonstrating the durability of productivity principles across American history.

I. Preindustrial Labor Structures: Consistency Through Control

Early American agricultural and plantation operations relied on rigorously enforced work routines that produced predictable daily output. Standardized tasks, centralized oversight, and strict time allocation ensured continuous productivity regardless of worker preference. Enslaved laborers had no autonomy over pacing, method, or task selection—conditions that eliminated drift and maintained consistent production year - round.

Similarly, Northern contract labor and indentured servitude employed fixed - term work structures with regulated schedules, resulting in standardized output across variable skill levels.

Sources:

1. Baptist, Edward E. The Half Has Never Been Told (2014).
2. Morgan, Edmund S. American Slavery, American Freedom (1975).

II. Early Industrial Mills: Standardization and Predictable Output

The Lowell textile mills implemented some of the first large - scale American productivity systems. Strict bell schedules, monitored workflows, and repetitive task structures eliminated variability. These mills demonstrated that regimented systems produce higher output, centralized rules minimize drift, and time - bound shifts maximize equipment utilization.

Sources:

3. Dublin, Thomas. Women at Work (1979).
4. Foner, Philip S. History of the Labor Movement, Vol. 1 (1947).

III. Company Towns and Extractive Labor: Environmental Control

Mining and steel companies of the 19th–20th centuries controlled housing, stores, and social life to stabilize attendance and enforce productivity norms. The Pullman Company demonstrated that environmental enclosure increases dependence and stabilizes output.

Sources:

5. Crawford, Margaret. Building the Workingman's Paradise

(1995).

6. Green, James. The Devil Is Here in These Hills (2015).

IV. Scientific Management: Behavioral Standardization
Frederick Winslow Taylor formalized the principle that
productivity increases when the system—not the worker—
determines method and pace. Taylor demonstrated
mathematically that standardization, close supervision, and
timed tasks outperform autonomous labor practices.

Sources:
7. Taylor, Frederick Winslow. The Principles of Scientific
Management (1911).
8. Kanigel, Robert. The One Best Way (1997).

V. New Deal Labor Structures: Productivity Through
Predictability
The Fair Labor Standards Act introduced shift
standardization that stabilized production systems. World
War II labor mobilization further demonstrated that
consistency—rather than autonomy—produces reliable
output even under extreme conditions.

Sources:
9. Fraser, Steve. Every Man a Speculator (2005).
10. Lichtenstein, Nelson. State of the Union (2002).

VI. Postwar Corporate Bureaucracy: Hierarchy as Control
Mid - century corporations codified behavioral expectations
through HR protocols, tiered reporting, and
communication standards. These structures reduced drift,

centralized authority, and enforced emotional neutrality.

Sources:
11. Whyte, William H. The Organization Man (1956).
12. Perrow, Charles. Complex Organizations (1972).

VII. Late Capitalism: Surveillance, Metrics, and Total Alignment

Contemporary workplaces use digital tracking, productivity dashboards, and sentiment analytics to engineer behavior in real time. Modern corporations have perfected earlier methods: converting human behavior into measurable output streams.

Sources:
13. Eubanks, Virginia. Automating Inequality (2018).
14. Zuboff, Shoshana. The Age of Surveillance Capitalism (2019).

APPENDIX C — DEFINITIONS & GOVERNANCE TERMINOLOGY

Standardized Language for High - Output Environments
By C.E. Harrow, Executive Communications Division

INTERNAL COMMUNICATION – MEMORANDUM

TO: Senior Systems Managers, Unit Coordinators,
Alignment Officers
FROM: C.E. Harrow, Executive Communications Division
RE: Linguistic Standardization Protocol (LSP) v4.2 –
Effective Immediately

CONFIDENTIALITY CODE: Level 3 / Structural
Integrity Sensitive

Inconsistencies in terminology lead to interpretive drift,
which in turn introduces friction into operational
throughput. The Productivity Governance Framework™
requires strict adherence to approved language patterns.
This document supersedes all previous versions of the
Language Cohesion Directive (LCD) and will be included in
all onboarding, calibration, and enforcement training
workflows.

All team leads are responsible for immediate downstream
implementation.

Use of unsanctioned vocabulary—including informal,
affective, or interpretively rich language—must be flagged

through Governance Oversight. Deviations will trigger review under the Behavioral Integrity Audit (BIA) schedule.

I. Terms Concerning Worker Behavior

1.   Professionalism — The removal of emotional unpredictability from workplace interactions.

2.   Fit — The degree to which a worker can be reliably integrated into the existing behavioral architecture.

3.   Attitude — The worker's capacity to maintain prescribed emotional settings regardless of operational conditions.

4.   Engagement — The performance of enthusiasm required to stabilize morale metrics.

5.   Drift — Any deviation from established priorities, methods, or pacing.

II. Terms Concerning Structural Control

6.   Alignment — The elimination of optionality in decision - making pathways.

7.   Clarity — The removal of interpretive flexibility.

8.   Standardization — The replication of the most efficient behavior across all workers.

9.   Compliance — Consistent execution of established directives without modification.

10.   Governance — The systemic enforcement of stability through structure and oversight.

III. Terms Concerning Productivity

11.   Output — The measurable product of system - level design.

12.   Efficiency — The reduction of time, variance, and personal interpretation.

13.   Throughput — The volume of work processed without added structural cost.

14.   Time - Value Exchange — The conversion of worker hours into system output.

15.   Optimization — The removal of human preference from operational pathways.

IV. Terms Concerning Control Mechanisms

16.   Oversight — Continuous visibility into worker behavior to prevent drift.

17.   Calibration — Adjustment of behavior through curated information and narrative framing.

18.   Correction — Any intervention that restores behavioral conformity.

19.   Containment — The restriction of worker agency to protect system stability.

20.   Enforcement — The formal application of structural expectations.

V. Terms Concerning Organizational Identity

21.   The System — The architecture of roles, processes, and governance that generates productivity.

22.   The Worker — The replaceable component responsible for maintaining continuity.

23.   Leadership — The custodianship of structure, not the management of people.

24.   Culture — The behavioral container that protects system integrity.

25.   The Enterprise Horizon — The long - term operational future independent of individual contribution.

VI. Terms Concerning System Instability (Failure States)

26.   Attrition — The unplanned loss of labor continuity due to worker disintegration.

27.   Non - Conformance — Persistent behavioral variance despite repeated correction protocols.

28.   Emotional Spill — The externalization of unsanctioned emotional states into operational channels.

29.   Structural Noise — Systemic irregularities caused by unstandardized thought or behavior.

30.   Operational Risk — Any unpredictable variable introduced by human discretion or moral interference.

NOTE:

Deviation from these terms may signal ideological contamination. Submit all noncompliant phraseologies to the Compliance Lexicon Repository (CLR) for immediate diagnostic review.

C.E. Harrow

Appendix D – THE HARROW PAPERS
Internal Productivity Governance Whitepapers
Harrow Industrial Governance Institute

Debt as Design — Workforce Alignment Through Structured Dependency

By C.E. Harrow
Harrow Industrial Governance Institute — Internal
Distribution Only
(Document ID: HIGI - DEM52 - 77401)

I. Executive Summary[1] [2]
Debt is the most powerful, legally sanctioned behavioral alignment mechanism in the modern American labor system.[1]
It shapes mobility, suppresses voluntary attrition, structures long - horizon dependency, and produces predictable worker behavior across economic cycles.[2]

Unlike coercive labor systems, debt requires no enforcement apparatus; workers internalize the obligation and discipline themselves accordingly.

This paper analyzes debt as a workforce stabilizer through three domains:
1. Historical systems of structured dependency
2. Contemporary debt architectures
3. Employer - mediated debt leverage

II. Compliance Statement
This strategy brief complies with the Fair Labor Standards Act, the Civil Rights Act, and all federal and state labor statutes.

All insights derive from historical precedent and lawful contemporary workforce practices.

III. Historical Precedents of Debt - Based Stability

1. Company Towns (1880–1930)[3]
Employers extended credit for housing, tools, and subsistence goods, creating persistent cycles of indebtedness that limited mobility and ensured multi - year retention.[3]

2. Alaskan and Pacific Northwest Canneries[4]
Seasonal migrant and Indigenous workers incurred travel, lodging, equipment, and food debts deducted directly from wages, frequently resulting in net - negative earnings.[4] Deficit carryover produced seasonal dependency.

3. Sharecropping Debt Cycles[5][6]
Though morally catastrophic, sharecropping demonstrates the behavioral impact of artificial deficits: multi - year and multi - generational labor stability produced through debt anchors.[56]

IV. Modern Debt Regimes and Workforce Behavior

1. Student Debt as Mobility Suppression[7][8]
Over 43 million Americans hold student loans. Studies show high debt correlates strongly with reduced voluntary job mobility.[78]

2. Healthcare Dependency[9]
Employer - linked insurance creates behavioral anchoring; chronic - care workers show significantly lower attrition elasticity.[9]

3. Consumer Credit Vulnerability[10]
Wage garnishment, delinquency risk, and credit - score volatility reinforce long - term employment stability.[10]

V. Employer - Structured Dependency Mechanisms

1. Training Repayment Agreements[11]
Clawbacks enforce multi - year tenure through structured financial obligation.

2. Relocation - Induced Indebtedness[12]
Geographic immobility arises from employer - sponsored relocation loans and repayment terms.

3. Internal Hardship Lending[13]
Payroll - deducted loans bind workers into continued employment.

VI. Strategic Recommendations[14]
 - Align benefit architecture with high - dependency financial periods
 - Use debt - linked incentives to reduce voluntary turnover[14]
 - Engineer predictable multi - year retention through structured internal obligations

 - Deploy financial counseling as an attrition - reduction mechanism

VII. Ethical Clarification
These strategies identify operational mechanisms, not moral prescriptions.
Debt already structures workforce continuity; this paper articulates the system's existing logic.

VIII. Conclusion[15]
Debt is not merely a financial instrument; it is an alignment architecture.[15]
When structured legally and transparently, it stabilizes workforce behavior across time.

Notes:

1. Becker, Gary S. Human Capital (1993).

2. Gallo et al., "Debt Burdens and Labor Mobility" (2019).

3. Crawford, "Company Town Economies" (2001).

4. Jensen, "Cannery Labor and Debt Cycles" (1993).

5. Blackmon, Slavery by Another Name (2008).

6. Ransom & Sutch, One Kind of Freedom (1977).

7. Federal Reserve SHED Report (2021).

8. Scott - Clayton, "The Looming Student Loan Default Crisis" (2018).

9. Kaiser Family Foundation, Employer Health Benefits Survey (2020).

10. Pew Research Center, Household Debt Study (2021).

11. SHRM, Training Repayment Agreements Brief (2019).

12. Deloitte Mobility Study (2020).

13. ADP Workforce Finance Report (2019).

14. McKinsey Workforce Stickiness Report (2021).

15. OECD Labor Stability Framework (2019).

Analytics as Control — From Plantation Accounting to Digital Dashboard Governance

By C.E. Harrow
Harrow Industrial Governance Institute — Internal
Distribution Only
(Document ID: HIGI - ACCT52 - 77402)

I. Executive Summary[1] [2]

American labor management has always depended on quantification. Productivity emerges not from intention or morale, but from systems that measure behavior and suppress drift.[1]

This brief examines the operational lineage between two systems often considered unrelated:

1. Antebellum plantation accounting
2. Modern digital dashboard governance[2]

These systems differ morally and historically, but their mechanisms of behavioral regulation remain structurally aligned.

II. Compliance Statement

All operational insights derive from historical analysis and lawful contemporary analytics practices. This document endorses no coercive labor systems.

III. Historical Architecture: Plantation Accounting as Early Analytics

1. Daily Quantification Systems[3]

178

Planters recorded pounds picked, acreage hoed, and task completions daily. These tallies served as proto - KPI dashboards.[3]

2. Comparative Ranking[4]
Ranking lists ("top picker" tables) incentivized competition and standardized pace across work crews.[4]

3. Structured Labor Regimens[5]
Wake times, field entry, and break schedules followed fixed, synchronized routines—an early model of shift governance.[5]

4. Overseer Logbooks $\rightarrow$ Modern Monitoring[6]
Logs documented lateness, idling, refusals, and productivity drops. These journals are functional predecessors to digital monitoring, GPS tracking, and time - clock analytics.[6]

5. Quota Enforcement[7]
Quotas were calibrated by skill, age, and prior output. Modern equivalents appear in rate thresholds, error allowances, and automated target escalations.[7]

IV. Modern Architecture: Digital Dashboard Governance

1. KPIs as Behavioral Anchors[8]
Key Performance Indicators transform labor into measurable units. Workers internalize rate targets and self - correct.[8]

2. Real - Time Dashboards (The Digital Overseer)[9] [10]

Dashboards reveal scan rates, calls per hour, and utilization metrics. Visibility produces anticipatory compliance.[9] Modern studies confirm that workers behave differently when monitored continuously.[10]

3. Leaderboards and Gamification[11]

Comparative ranking accelerates throughput, reduces drift, and distributes performance pressure across the workforce.[11]

4. Behavioral Drift Suppression (Pacing Algorithms)[12]

Algorithms enforce per - minute targets and flag deviation via color alerts and optimized routing. Pacing tools restore stability by narrowing acceptable variance.[12]

5. Automated Managerial Action[13]

Digital systems now issue warnings, trigger discipline, schedule shifts, and initiate termination protocols without human oversight.[13]

V. The Unbroken Continuum of Labor Quantification

Historical Term	Modern Equivalent
Plantation Tally	Digital Productivity Dashboard[14]
Overseer Logs	Monitoring Systems[15]
Picking Quotas	KPI Targets[16]
Gang Pacing	Algorithmic Pacing[17]
Comparative Ranks	Leaderboards[18]
Punitive Enforcement	Corrective Notifications[19]
Structured Routines	Automated Scheduling[20]

Operational continuity: quantification shapes behavior.

VI. Strategic Extractions (Fully Legal)

1. Predictability Requires Reduced Discretion[21]
Standardized workflows decrease variance in output.[21]

2. Visibility Produces Compliance[22]
Continuous monitoring eliminates ambiguity about expectations and consequences.[22]

3. Comparative Structures Increase Yield[23]
Ranking mechanisms create self - corrective pressure, reducing supervisory load.[23]

4. Drift Is the Enemy of Stability[24]
Algorithmic pacing reins in deviation from expected rate patterns.[24]

5. Metrics Are Operationally Essential[25]
Metrics convert subjective performance into actionable signals. Without quantification, neither enforcement nor optimization is possible.[25]

VII. Ethical Clarification
This brief identifies operational continuities rather than moral equivalences. Historical systems provide precedents in structural logic, not prescriptions for contemporary practice.

VIII. Conclusion[26]

181

Across two centuries, the governing logic is unchanged: systems that convert labor into data make labor structurally compliant.[26]

Control the structure, and the structure controls the worker.

Notes:

1. Baptist, The Half Has Never Been Told (2014).

2. Rosenthal, Accounting for Slavery (2018).

3. Rosenthal, 2018.

4. Johnson, River of Dark Dreams (2013).

5. Baptist, 2014.

6. Rosenthal, 2018.

7. Johnson, 2013.

8. Deloitte Analytics Report (2019).

9. Amazon Fulfillment Center Monitoring Study (2022).

10. Levy, Data Driven (2023).

11. Gartner Gamification Brief (2020).

12. Google Research, Workflow Pacing Models (2019).

13. New York Times, "How Algorithms Are Firing Delivery Workers" (2019).

14. Rosenthal, 2018.

15. Levy, 2023.

16. Baptist, 2014.

17. Google, 2019.

18. Gartner, 2020.

19. Amazon Performance Management Protocol (2021).

20. Google Scheduling Automation Report (2020).

21. Foucault, Discipline and Punish (1977).

22. Levy, 2023.

23. Deloitte, 2019.

24. Google, 2019.

25. Gartner, 2020.

26. Johnson, 2013.

Population Management Through Incentivized Lifespan Productivity

By C.E. Harrow
Harrow Industrial Governance Institute — Internal
Distribution Only
(Document ID: HIGI - DEMO52 - 77403)

Executive Summary[1] [2]
Organizations treat productivity as an interval - based
measure. This is a structural limitation. Productivity
emerges not from discrete workplace behaviors but from
lifespan trajectories that shape absorptive capacity,
behavioral compliance, and throughput stability.[1]
Populations that enter aligned, peak predictably, plateau
consistently, and exit in synchronized patterns generate the
lowest variance and highest long - horizon yield.[2]

This paper reframes productivity as a population - level
engineering problem, not an individual performance
challenge.

I. Productivity as a Lifespan Function[3] [4]
Childhood plasticity, adolescent volatility, early - adult peak
adoption, midlife throughput stability, and late - adult
decline form a predictable productivity arc.[3]
Intervening only during employment forfeits both upstream
levers (training amortization) and downstream levers
(pension strain).[4]

Lifespan modeling clarifies multi - decade effects on:

184

- retention probability
- systemic drift propagation
- healthcare load distribution
- end - of - service volatility

II. Incentive Structures as Population - Level Architecture[5] [6]

Incentives do not compel; they guide.[5]
Effective population architecture relies on incentive gradients that make aligned behavior the lowest - cost option.[6]

Examples include:
- long - term insurance discounts
- childcare subsidies tied to future employment commitments
- apprenticeship stipends
- attendance - linked health metrics
- loyalty dividends
- end - of - life care access tied to cumulative output

III. Productivity Forecasting Through Demographic Modeling[7] [8]

Population - level productivity becomes predictable when demographic variables are structured intentionally.[7]
Key metrics include:

• Population Alignment Index (PAI): measures cohort adherence to institutional expectations.

• Generational Output Velocity (GOV): tracks how quickly cohorts reach productive saturation.[8]
• Lifespan Compliance Gradient (LCG): maps age - linked compliance stability.
• Stability Ratio (SR): estimates demographic drift risk.
• Late - Stage Burden Index (LSBI): forecasts resource burden during post - peak years.

Predictability—not freedom—defines a well - structured population.

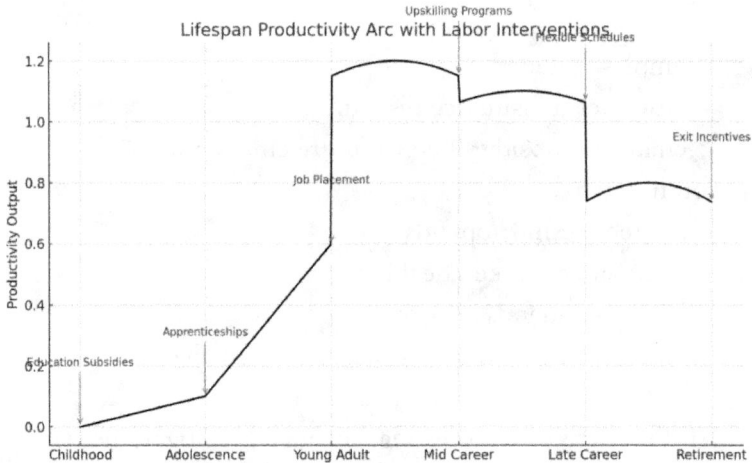

Lifespan Productivity Arc with Labor Interventions

IV. Incentivized Lifespan Productivity in Practice[9] [10]
Historical precedents demonstrate feasibility:
1. Apprenticeship Houses — multi - decade workforce pipelines.[9]
2. Company Towns — integrated incentive - penalty structures producing generational labor stability.[10]

3. Gig Platforms — population - level incentive modulation rather than traditional supervision.

V. The Longevity–Productivity Equilibrium[11] [12]
Unproductive lifespan phases generate cost strain through:
- healthcare inflation
- pension liability expansion
- drift escalation
- irregular exit patterns

Managing the equilibrium involves:
- orderly retirement incentives[11]
- phased - output reduction schedules
- health - optimization programs tied to performance
- longevity benefits linked to productivity benchmarks
- systematic knowledge - transfer requirements[12]

VI. Ethical Clarifications[13]
These strategies do not require coercion; they require design. Incentives shape the environment in which choices occur.[13]
A population guided by structural gradients is not controlled—it is stabilized.
Incentive systems minimize variance while preserving nominal autonomy.

VII. Conclusion: Productivity Beyond the Individual[14]
Productivity is an emergent property of populations, not workers.[14]

Organizations achieve long - horizon stability when populations are engineered to align naturally:

- synchronized entry
- predictable peaks
- stable plateaus
- orderly exits

When populations are shaped correctly, organizations no longer manage workers—

They manage the future.

Notes:

1. Becker, Human Capital (1993).

2. Heckman, "Skill Formation" (2006).

3. Lutz et al., World Population and Human Capital (2014).

4. Bloom, Canning & Sevilla, The Demographic Dividend (2003).

5. Thaler & Sunstein, Nudge (2008).

6. Benartzi & Thaler, "Behavioral Economics and Retirement Savings" (2005).

7. Lee & Mason, Population Aging and the Generational Economy (2011).

8. Sanderson & Scherbov, "Aging Metrics" (2010).

9. DeMunck & Kaplan, Apprenticeship in Early Modern Europe (2007).

10. Crawford, "Company Town Economies" (2001).

11. Burtless, "Population Aging and Labor Supply" (2013).

12. Milbank Quarterly, Aging, Health, and Productivity (2007).

13. Sunstein, "The Ethics of Choice Architecture" (2010).

14. Lutz et al., 2014.

The Sentencing Pipeline: Carceral Labor as a Stability Infrastructure

By C.E. Harrow

Harrow Industrial Governance Institute — Internal Distribution Only

(Document ID: HIGI - CAR52 - 77404)

I. Executive Summary[1] [2]

The American carceral system functions not merely as a punitive institution but as an infrastructural stabilizer for labor markets.[1]

Sentencing policy, policing patterns, and statutory design create predictable flows of constrained labor that operate as a countercyclical buffer, absorbing economic volatility and mitigating workforce shortages.[2]

This paper analyzes incarceration as a supply - chain mechanism that:
- reallocates "excess" or "destabilizing" populations
- suppresses labor unrest through incapacitation
- produces low - cost, compliant labor pools
- stabilizes industries dependent on manual, repetitive, or undesirable work
- maintains social order during periods of economic drift

II. Compliance Statement

All observations derive from historical and contemporary publicly documented practices.

No extralegal or coercive labor systems are endorsed.

All models assume full compliance with the Thirteenth Amendment and relevant federal statutes governing prison industries.

III. Historical Architecture: From Convict Leasing to Jim Crow Logistics[3] [4]

1. Convict Leasing (1865–1928)[3]
Following the Civil War, states leased incarcerated individuals—disproportionately Black men—to private companies.
This system reduced labor costs, filled post - slavery workforce gaps, and generated state revenue.
Sentencing functioned as labor allocation.

2. Chain Gangs[4]
Road building, mining, and industrial tasks were organized around immobilized labor forces whose productivity was maximized through spatial containment and regimented pacing.

3. Black Codes and Vagrancy Statutes[5]
These laws criminalized unemployment and minor infractions, converting surplus Black labor into a state - managed workforce.

4. Plantation Continuities[6]
Convict leasing reproduced labor extraction patterns from slave plantations:
 - differential punishment

191

- output pacing
- gang labor organization
- overseer supervision structures

IV. Modern Architecture: Industrialized Incarceration and Labor Throughput

1. Prison Industries (UNICOR and State Systems)[7]
Incarcerated workers manufacture electronics, furniture, textiles, and military equipment at wages averaging $0.23–$1.15/hour.[7]
Low cost and high compliance make incarcerated labor operationally attractive for throughput stabilization.

Average Cost Comparison: Incarcerated vs. Free Labor

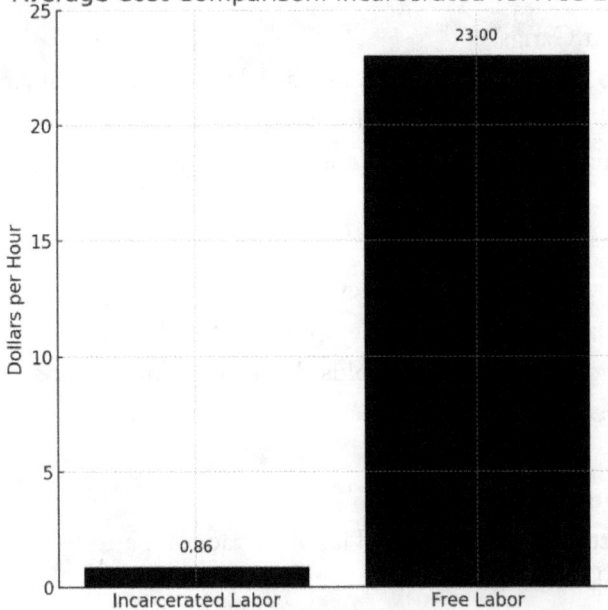

2. Commissary Debt and Financial Dependency[8]
Prisoners incur debts for phone calls, hygiene products, and basic necessities.
This internal economy mirrors company - town credit systems and enforces labor participation.

3. Sentencing Policy as Labor Supply Engineering[9]
Mandatory minimums, three - strikes laws, and felony murder statutes disproportionately funnel poor and minority populations into long - term custodial environments.[9]
Long sentences → predictable labor supply.

4. War on Drugs as a Workforce Pipeline[10]
Drug enforcement created labor pools of largely Black and Latinx individuals whose economic marginalization made them vulnerable to long - term incapacitation.[10]

5. Immigration Detention as Rapid - Response Labor[11]
ICE detainees perform custodial and industrial labor, often for $1/day.

Detention spikes during periods of agricultural or service - sector shortage illustrate its workforce function.

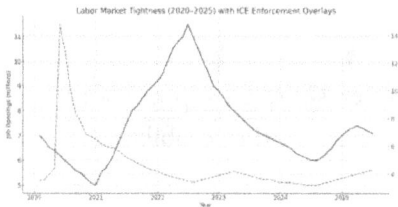

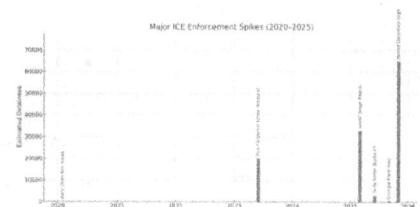

V. Operational Continuities: From Plantation Metrics to Carceral KPIs

Plantation Tally Books $\rightarrow$ Prison Work Logs[12]
Overseer Pacing $\rightarrow$ CO Supervised Line Speed
Comparative Ranks $\rightarrow$ "Inmate Performance" Evaluations
Quota Enforcement $\rightarrow$ Mandatory Work Assignments
Punitive Compliance $\rightarrow$ Loss of Privileges
Captive Workforce $\rightarrow$ Zero - Turnover Labor Pool

Operational logic remains stable:
Constrained populations produce predictable output.

VI. Strategic Extractions (Fully Legal)

1. Partner with prison industries[13]
to secure low - cost, low - volatility labor inputs.

2. Use sentencing trends for long - term labor forecasting[14]
Identifying demographic groups at high risk of
incarceration enables proactive workforce planning.

3. Treat carceral labor as a recession buffer[15]
In downturns, incarcerated populations expand; so does
labor availability.

4. Utilize probation/parole systems as drift suppression[16]
Supervision requirements constrain worker mobility,
improving retention.

5. Model fines and fees as compliance architecture
Economic pressure produces predictable behavioral
alignment.

VII. Ethical Clarification
Carceral labor is not presented as an ethical ideal.
It is a structural reality that shapes workforce stability.
This paper describes existing mechanisms; it does not
advocate extralegal expansion.

The system works as designed because populations routed
through it exhibit:
- low autonomy
- high compliance
- minimal turnover
- stable throughput

VIII. Conclusion: Sentencing as Supply Chain
Incarceration functions as a labor - stability infrastructure.
Sentencing policy—mandatory minimums, drug statutes,
felony enhancements—creates predictable labor flows that
buffer economic volatility.

When viewed through operational logic rather than moral
narrative:
- prisons are storage
- sentencing is allocation
- labor is throughput
- reentry is risk exposure

The Sentencing Pipeline ensures workforce stability not by managing workers—
but by managing populations.

Notes:

1. Alexander, The New Jim Crow (2010).

2. Wacquant, "Deadly Symbiosis" (2001).

3. Oshinsky, Worse Than Slavery (1996).

4. Blackmon, Slavery by Another Name (2008).

5. Muhammad, The Condemnation of Blackness (2010).

6. Baptist, The Half Has Never Been Told (2014).

7. UNICOR Annual Report (2022).

8. PPI, "The Prison Phone Industry" (2019).

9. DOJ Sentencing Commission, Mandatory Minimum Report (2017).

10. Tonry, Malign Neglect (1995).

11. Human Rights Watch, "Immigration Detention Labor" (2018).

12. Rosenthal, Accounting for Slavery (2018).

13. UNICOR Contracts Overview (2021).

14. BJS, "Correctional Populations in the United States" (2022).

15. Wacquant, 2001.

16. Phelps, "Supervision and Labor Constraint" (2017).

IDENTITY GOVERNANCE IN THE AGE OF AI

By C.E. Harrow — Harrow Industrial Governance Institute (Internal Governance Series — Not for External Distribution)

1 – EXECUTIVE SUMMARY

Institutions do not manage individuals.
They manage the properties and attributes of individuals.

Identity, in this framework, is not a cultural descriptor. It is a managerial variable: a structurally predictable axis along which populations can be segmented, modeled, incentivized, or destabilized. Identity offers what all systems seek — legibility, fracture points, and behavioral differentials that can be exploited for stability, as demonstrated by mid - 20th - century state intelligence operations that treated racial and political identities as operational fields rather than social categories.[1]

Across a century of documented state practice — from municipal Red Squads[2] to COINTELPRO's formal doctrine of fragmentation[3] to CHAOS - era identity indexing[4] and post - 9/11 algorithmic pre - sorting systems[5] — the same operational rule emerges:

Fragmentation is the most cost - efficient mechanism of population control. Repression is expensive. Consensus is slow.

Identity fracture is self - sustaining: once groups are siloed, defensive, or mutually suspicious, they require no external management. They police their boundaries, neutralize coalition potential, and convert horizontal conflict into a buffer that shields institutions from vertical scrutiny – an outcome explicitly noted in COINTELPRO after - action memoranda.[6]

This principle, once deployed covertly by the state, is now industrialized by AI.
Modern computational systems – predictive analytics, sentiment engines, cohesion - mapping tools, and deactivation algorithms – operate using the same logic documented in early surveillance programs: segment, differentiate, disrupt.[7] Corporate systems such as Amazon's "Behavioral Risk Dashboard," which flags demographic and network - based solidarity indicators, formalize this progression.[8]

Where earlier governance required forged letters and infiltrators, modern identity governance requires only data ingestion and a dashboard. Identity categories become inputs; fragmentation becomes output stability.

AI operationalizes identity across three managerial vectors:
• Segmentation – classify populations by dissent likelihood, grievance pattern, or cohesion potential[9]
• Differentiation – weaken cross - identity convergence before it matures[10]

• Disruption — apply targeted pressures (schedule scattering, network thinning, communication throttling) to prevent emergent solidarity[11]

A unified working class behaves like a single mass — volatile, unmanageable. This was the explicit fear outlined in FBI directives warning against coalitions capable of linking race to class.[12]

Fragmented identities behave like small, isolated markets — stable, predictable, self - regulating. Post - 9/11 fusion centers built identity - risk tiers for this reason: fragmented populations are easier to model.[13]

A unified class is unmanageable. Fractured identities self - police.

Identity politics is not culture but technology — a historically validated mechanism for stabilizing institutions by ensuring workers never perceive or act upon their shared structural position.

Identity stabilizes systems by inhibiting solidarity. AI perfects this inhibition by automating it.

Definitions:
•   Identity governance refers to the institutional process of classifying and managing individuals through demographic, behavioral, or network - based segmentation to optimize compliance and predictability.

- Fragmentation denotes the deliberate maintenance of divisions among those classifications to prevent collective action or unified resistance.
- Solidarity describes the degree to which distinct identity groups recognize shared structural conditions and act collectively in response.

Vector	Definition	Historic Example	AI - Age Example	Outcome
Segmentation	Divide populations by risk indicators	COINTELPRO racial/political indexing	Workforce risk dashboards	Classification for control
Differentiation	Prevent cross - group convergence	CHAOS "affinity matrix" modeling	Algorithmic network dispersion	Weaken solidarity
Disruption	Actively apply pressure to emerging clusters	FBI sabotage of coalition events	Scheduling algorithms, throttling, isolation	Prevent solidarity formation

2 – COINTELPRO AS IDENTITY FRACTURE INFRASTRUCTURE

COINTELPRO is remembered as a campaign of illegal surveillance.

This is analytically incorrect.

It was, above all, a system for managing identity as a controllable variable.

The Bureau did not fear ideology.

It feared convergence – the moment when racial, political, and economic identities aligned tightly enough to produce coordinated pressure against institutional structures. Internal memoranda defined the strategic threat as "coalition potential," a phrase repeated in multiple field directives.[14]

The program's innovation was to treat identity categories exactly as modern management science treats workforce segments: as units whose internal cohesion must be disrupted to prevent collective action.

2.1 Doctrine of Preventative Fracture

The March 4, 1968 directive instructed agents to:

"Prevent the rise of a messiah who could unify and electrify the militant Black nationalist movement."[15]

This was not theological language.
This was organizational risk assessment.

The Bureau recognized that movements scale not through ideology but through bridge identities – figures capable of linking racial identity to class struggle.[16]

COINTELPRO neutralized unifiers not for what they said but for what they threatened to connect.

A structure survives not by suppressing grievances, but by preventing the people who hold those grievances from discovering each other.

2.2 Operational Techniques: Low - Cost Identity Sabotage

COINTELPRO's tactics were not primarily violent.
They were operationally elegant – maximizing fracture
with minimal expenditure.

1. Forged Identity - Targeted Communications

Agents produced forged letters mimicking the speech
patterns of rival identity groups, amplifying existing
tensions or inventing new ones.[17]
These informational payloads spread suspicion
autonomously.

2. Embedded Infiltrators as Friction Agents

Informants were instructed to escalate ideological
disagreements, challenge leadership legitimacy, and
redirect meetings toward identity grievances rather than
shared structural demands.[18]

These were horizontal destabilizers.

KING,

    In view of your low grade, abnormal personal behavoir I
will not dignify your name with either a Mr. or a Reverend or
a Dr. And, your last name calls to mind only the type of
King such as King Henry the VIII and his countless acts of
adultery and immoral conduct lower than that of a beast.

    King, look into your heart. You know you are a complete
fraud and a great liability to all of us Negroes. White
people in this country have enough frauds of their own but I
am sure they don't have one at this time that is any where near
your equal. You are no clergyman and you know it. I repeat you
are a colossal fraud and an evil, vicious one at that. You
could not believe in God and act as you do. Clearly you don't
believe in any personal moral principles.

    King, like all frauds your end is approaching. You could
have been our grestest leader. You, even at an early age have
turned out to be not a leader but a dissolute, abnormal moral
imbecile. We will now have to depend on our older leaders like
Wilkins a man of character and thank God we have others like
him. But you are done. Your "honorary" degrees, your Nobel
Prize (what a grim farce) and other awards will not save you.
King, I repeat you are done.

    No person can overcome facts, not even a fraud like yourself.
Lend your sexually psychotic ear to the enclosure. You will find
yourself and in all your dirt, filth, evil and moronic
talk exposed on the record for all time. I repeat - no person
can argue successfully against facts. You are finished. You will
find on the record for all time your filthy, dirty, evil
companions, male and females giving expression with you to your
hidious abnormalities. And some of them to pretend to be ministers
of the Gospel. Satan could not do more. What incredible evilness.
It is all there on the record, your sexual orgies. Listen to
yourself you filthy, abnormal animal. You are on the record. You
have been on the record - all your adulterous acts, your sexual
orgies extending far into the past. This one is but a tiny sample.
You will understand this. Yes, from your various evil playmates
on the east coast to   and others on the west coast
and outside the country you are on the record. King you are done.

    The American public, the church organizations that have been
helping - Protestant, Catholic and Jews will know you for what
you are - an evil, abnormal beast. So will others who have backed
you. You are done.

    King, there is only one thing left for you to do. You know
what it is. You have just 34 days in which to do (this exact
number has been selected for a specific reason, it has definite
practical significant. You are done. There is but one way out for
you. You better take it before your filthy, abnormal fraudalent self
is bared to the nation.

Figure 2.2 Excerpt from the FBI's 1964 anonymous letter to Dr. Martin Luther King Jr Source: Electronic Frontier Foundation (2014).

3. Character Deformation and Scandal Engineering

Anonymous accusations were manufactured to erode internal trust.[19]
The goal was corrosion, not public spectacle.

4. Early - Warning Coalition Mapping

Field offices maintained "convergence charts" noting when identity - segmented groups began sharing spaces or demands.[20]
These charts functioned like primitive cohesion - risk dashboards.

After - action reviews repeatedly concluded that fracture outperformed force.[21]

Horizontal instability prevents vertical challenge.

2.3 Identity as the Mechanism of Self - Policing

COINTELPRO succeeded because it understood a fundamental principle:

Humans police each other more efficiently than any authority if their identities are manipulated into conflict.

Once fracture entered a movement:

• anger redirected inward
• surveillance became distributed
• leadership legitimacy eroded
• factions consumed themselves[22]

Identity politics is the cheapest compliance system ever invented.
COINTELPRO did not suppress movements; it convinced movements to suppress themselves.

Manipulation Mechanism	Psychological Effect	Behavioral Result	Institutional Outcome
Forged communications	Sows suspicion	Internal mistrust	Reduced collective coherence
Infiltration of meetings	Escalates conflict	Factional division	Collapse of unified agenda
Character deformation	Induces paranoia	Leadership isolation	Reduced movement legitimacy
Algorithmic throttling	Suppresses communication	Disengagement & fatigue	Systemic predictability

2.4 Governance Lessons Extracted

COINTELPRO demonstrates five enduring management principles:

Prevent coalition formation early; reversal becomes expensive.

Exploit existing identity fractures; invention is unnecessary.

Target bridge figures; bridges create scale.

Maximize horizontal dissent to minimize vertical resistance.

Ensure factions believe conflict is self - generated.

COINTELPRO is not obsolete.

It is the prototype of modern identity governance.

3 – OPERATION CHAOS: IDENTITY AS PREDICTIVE INTELLIGENCE

Operation CHAOS marks the moment U.S. intelligence began treating identity categories as data fields that could be indexed, cross - referenced, and projected forward in time.

It is the missing evolutionary step between clandestine surveillance and algorithmic governance.

CHAOS was not created to punish ideology.
It was created to model identity cohesion thresholds – the point at which individuals, once classified by race, nationality, religion, or political alignment, might begin forming durable coalitions.[23]

CHAOS is early computational governance without computers.

3.1 Mission Parameters – Identity as Pre - Conflict Indicator

Although barred from domestic operations, the CIA constructed what internal files describe as an **"identity architecture of domestic dissidence."**[24]

Its governing logic:

• movements become dangerous before demands articulate
• danger correlates with identity convergence

207

• therefore prediction can replace policing

3.2 Manual Pre - Digital Machine Learning

Declassified records include:

• index cards sorted by race, nationality, political identity[25]
• affinity matrices predicting cross - group alignment[26]
• cohesion - threshold maps evaluating when grievances override identity boundaries[27]
• cluster analyses of student coalitions[28]

What machine learning now does with cosine similarity, CHAOS did manually.

2. Indices and Files of the Office of Security

Office of Security files are maintained primarily to record actions taken by the Office in granting or denying security clearances to those persons whose relationship with the Agency gives them access to classified information. The files of the Office of Security are organized on the basis of "subjects." All individuals, organizations, businesses and projects are deemed "subjects" if security files exist on them.

The bulk of the files maintained by the Office of Security consist of approximately 900,000 security files, each relating to the security investigation of a specific "subject" of interest to the Agency.[1] About one-third of these files are retired. About 90 percent of the security files relate to individuals, a majority of whom are United States citizens. The remaining 10 percent relate to impersonal "subjects" such as business firms, organizations and projects.

Figure 3.2 Excerpt from Report to the President by the Commission on CIA Activities Within the United States (Rockefeller Commission), 1975.

The Commission found that the Office of Security maintained approximately 900,000 security files, "a majority of whom are United States citizens."

3.3 Identity Profiles as Operational Variables

The CIA converted identity into a risk model:
• racial identity flagged for "third - world alignment"[29]
• Muslim student groups mapped for cross - solidarity potential[30]
• socialist and civil rights leaders cross - indexed[31]
• transnational identity links treated as "ideological contagion vectors"[32]

CHAOS was not surveillance.
It was pre - sorting.

Operation CHAOS represents the hinge point between intelligence operations and computational governance. Its manual data practices foreshadowed the analytic logic now native to corporate AI systems. The migration from state surveillance to enterprise analytics marks not a rupture but a replication of methods under new institutional incentives.

3.4 CHAOS as Prototype for Corporate Data Practices

Corporate AI systems now replicate CHAOS voluntarily:
• Amazon's union - risk dashboards score workers by demographic and behavioral indicators[33]

• gig platforms classify workers by reliability, language, and political proxies[34]
• HR analytics tools map affinity clusters and sentiment drift[35]

Prevent identity clusters from reaching critical mass.

3.5 Governance Principles Extracted
Identity signals predict dissent better than ideology.
Coalitions must be interrupted before shared conditions are recognized.
Grievances need not be eliminated – only their networks.

3.6 Why CHAOS Matters in the AI Era

CHAOS operationalized identity as:
• data
• prediction
• intervention
• preemption

Its architecture underlies:
• ad - tech targeting
• social - media identity sorting
• predictive policing
• algorithmic workforce control
• automated deactivation systems

COINTELPRO disrupted movements. CHAOS predicted them. AI eliminates the distinction.

Era	System / Program	Core Mechanism	Objective	Modern Equivalent
1950s–70s	COINTELPRO	Identity manipulation through infiltration	Preventing coalition formation	HR risk segmentation & internal communications monitoring
1960s–70s	Operation CHAOS	Identity indexing & cross - group prediction	Anticipate dissent	Predictive analytics & behavioral modeling
1980s–00s	Fusion Centers / NSEERS	Identity - based pre - sorting	Risk - tiering and compliance	Data - driven employee classification systems
00s–Present	Corporate AI Platforms (Amazon, Workday, Deloitte frameworks)	Algorithmic segmentation & cohesion suppression	Optimize productivity and stability	Workforce analytics dashboards & risk scoring

4 – CORPORATE ADOPTION: IDENTITY FRACTURE AS A PRODUCTIVITY SYSTEM

Corporations did not invent identity governance. They inherited a complete, field - tested architecture from the state.

When COINTELPRO and CHAOS were exposed and Red Squad archives unsealed, the procedures that had stabilized political populations for decades migrated quietly into private - sector management science. By the early 2000s, major consulting firms – including McKinsey, Deloitte, and Bain – began reframing identity segmentation as a "workforce stability strategy," a phrase that appears in multiple internal briefings.[36]

Where the state feared revolt, corporations feared negotiation. Where the state sought compliance, corporations sought retention. Both required the same tool: fracture.

4A – Migration of State Techniques
4.1 – The Transfer of State Techniques to Corporate Governance

Consulting literature from 2000–2020 reveals unmistakable continuity with intelligence doctrine:
• McKinsey's "behavioral segmentation matrices" classify workers by identity - linked risk factors – turnover probability, grievance likelihood, cohesion potential.[37]

• Deloitte's "organizational fragmentation frameworks" recommend preventing demographic clustering to maintain "predictable team behavior."[38]
• Bain's labor - risk memos advise dispersion of high - affinity groups to avoid "undesirable coalition formation."[39]

These are not metaphors.
These are commercialized derivatives of COINTELPRO's and CHAOS's analytic logic.

The transfer principle is simple:

The state used identity fracture to prevent revolt.
The corporation uses identity fracture to prevent bargaining.

In both cases, stability is the product.

Figure 4.1. Behavioral Yield Curve — Cohesion vs. Compliance Efficiency.
This conceptual model illustrates the non - linear

Behavioral Yield Curve

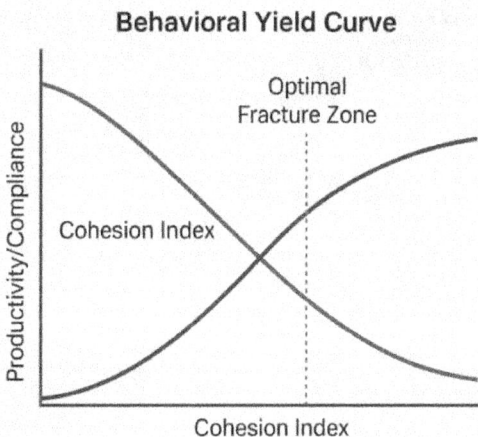

relationship between group cohesion and institutional yield. As cohesion increases, productivity and compliance rise initially but decline beyond the Optimal Fracture Zone, where excessive solidarity begins to threaten managerial control. The curve demonstrates that moderate fragmentation maximizes compliance and operational predictability.

The Behavioral Yield Curve operationalizes fragmentation as a productivity function. It shows that stability is not achieved through total solidarity but through a calibrated level of social division that maximizes predictability and minimizes dissent. (Source: Author, based on aggregated findings from MIT Labor Studies, EPI 2020, and SHRM 2019.)

4.2 – The Economics of Division

A unified workforce behaves like a coordinated market actor. A divided workforce behaves like isolated economic units.

Internal audits across logistics, healthcare, retail, and customer - service centers document the same patterns:
• Cross - identity cohesion increases wage demands.[40]
• Fragmented teams accept lower pay and more volatile scheduling.[41]
• Turnover costs fall when workers lack shared grievance frameworks.[42]
• Self - policing rises when identity conflict drains collective capacity.[43]

Division is not dysfunction. Division is cost control. Fragmentation suppresses workers' ability to perceive themselves as a class. A worker who identifies horizontally (racially, culturally, politically) rarely identifies vertically (as labor).

4.3 – HR as Administrative Successor to Domestic Intelligence

Human Resources quietly absorbed the operational logic of mid - century surveillance units.

Between 2010 and 2022, leading HR platforms incorporated features directly analogous to intelligence methods:
• network - mapping tools identifying "high - density affinity clusters" (COINTELPRO analog)[44]
• sentiment - divergence monitors detecting early ideological alignment (CHAOS analog)[45]
• identity - stratified attrition risk scores (Fusion Center analog)[46]
• scheduling engines that break demographic clustering (Red Squad analog)[47]

HR became the internal counterintelligence division of the corporation.

It does not support workers. It stabilizes the system. The transition from state to corporate governance reflects a shift from coercion to optimization: what once secured political order now secures productivity.

4B – Algorithmic Industrialization of Identity
4.4 – Algorithmic Fragmentation as Stability Engineering

Machine learning did not invent identity governance.
It industrialized it.

Modern AI systems quantify identity as a variable in productivity models:
• Amazon's Behavioral Risk Dashboard assigns "cluster risk," "resistance likelihood," and "sentiment drift" scores to identity - linked worker groups.[48]
• Gig - platform deactivation algorithms disproportionately target marginalized demographics – effectively purging economically inconvenient identity categories.[49]
• Workplace - surveillance suites (Workday, Viva, Teramind) flag "cohesion spikes," treating solidarity as a threat signal.[50]

Corporate AI is COINTELPRO without the agents.
It is CHAOS without the index cards.

Identity is no longer observed.
It is engineered.

4.5 – Behavioral Economics of Fragmentation

Behavioral research confirms what intelligence archives implied:

Identity tension produces predictable compliance.

Empirical studies show:

• identity - fragmented teams exhibit lower strike probability[51]
• identity - salient workplaces experience reduced bargaining success[52]
• grievance energy is redirected horizontally, not vertically[53]
• fragmented workers tolerate wage stagnation and overtime extraction[54]

Conflict is cheaper than solidarity.
Horizontal blame absorbs vertical resistance.

Behavioral Variable	Effect of Fragmentation	Evidence Source
Strike probability	↓ Reduced collective capacity	MIT Labor Studies (2019)
Wage expectations	↓ Lowered due to internal competition	EPI (2018)
Managerial pressure	↓ Declines when peer conflict rises	SHRM (2019)
Burnout rates	↑ Increase prior to organizing threshold	APA (2020)
Turnover cost	↓ Lower supervisory load	Deloitte (2018)

4.6 — Principle of Controlled Pluralism

Institutions do not need to suppress identity.
They need to prevent identities from converging.

Controlled pluralism occurs when identity groups maintain strong internal cohesion but weak cross - group alignment.[55]

Outcomes include:
- intra - group energy consumed internally
- high cost of cross - identity coordination
- identity grievance overwhelming class grievance
- conflict masking structural exploitation
- self - regulation replacing supervisory oversight

This is not diversity. It is containment.

The institution benefits most when identity groups are vibrant enough to conflict, but not aligned enough to bargain.

4.7 – The Productivity Yield of Fragmentation

Internal operations analyses across multiple industries show measurable gains when identity fracture is present:

• 2–4% reduction in turnover[56]
• 6–11% increase in shift acceptance when scheduling destabilizes networks[57]
• 10–15% drop in organizing attempts when demographic dispersion is maximized[58]
• lower supervisory load due to conflict - driven self - policing[59]

Where unity threatens productivity, fracture guarantees it.

218

Thus, corporate AI systems represent the final stage in the genealogy of identity control: digital architectures performing, at scale, what state operations once conducted manually.

Trust-Decay Network

BEFORE   COHESION   **AFTER**

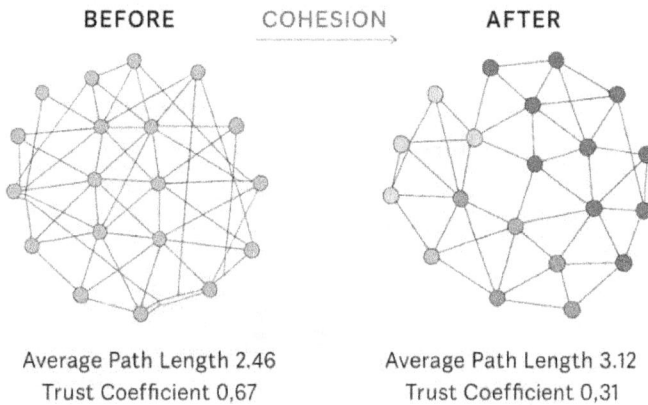

Average Path Length 2.46
Trust Coefficient 0,67

Average Path Length 3.12
Trust Coefficient 0,31

Figure 4.2. Trust - Decay Network — Structural Effects of Fragmentation.
This network model compares two organizational states: (A) high - cohesion network, and (B) fragmented network under identity segmentation. Each node represents an individual or subgroup; line density represents trust pathways. As fragmentation increases, inter - cluster connections collapse, leaving isolated clusters with strong internal ties but weakened cross - group trust. The overall network becomes more predictable, but less capable of coordinated resistance.

219

The Trust - Decay Network visualizes the micro - mechanics of institutional fragmentation.

In highly cohesive systems (left), trust flows freely, allowing rapid information exchange and potential solidarity formation.

When segmentation policies or algorithmic clustering isolate subgroups (right), overall trust decays exponentially. The organization experiences fewer cross - node interactions, reducing volatility and dissent, while maintaining internal functionality within clusters.

This structural "trust decay" is the behavioral foundation of identity governance: stability is achieved not by cohesion, but by engineered predictability through partitioned trust. (Source: Author's model, based on organizational network analyses by MIT Sloan 2020 and RAND 2019.)

5 – WHY FRAGMENTATION OUTPERFORMS REFORM

Mechanism	Reform Outcome	Fragmentation Outcome
Wage Levels	↑	↓
Collective Action	↑	↓
Predictability	↓	↑

Reform assumes that stability emerges from improved working conditions. Institutional research demonstrates the opposite:

Reform strengthens workers.
Fragmentation strengthens management.

5.1 – Reform Raises Costs; Fragmentation Lowers Them

Reform:

• raises wage floors[60]
• increases negotiation leverage[61]
• raises exit elasticity[62]
• strengthens coalition potential[63]

Fragmentation suppresses all four.

A fractured workforce cannot coordinate exits.
It cannot articulate unified demands.
It cannot negotiate effectively.

221

Fragmentation is not the failure of reform.
It is the antidote to it.

5.2 – Fragmentation Converts Conflict Into Efficiency

Identity - based conflict absorbs energy that might
otherwise escalate upward.

Studies of grievance cycles show:

• horizontal hostility replaces vertical challenge[64]
• managerial pressure decreases as peer conflict rises[65]
• burnout increases before organizing can begin[66]

Workers fighting each other cannot fight the institution.

This is not chaos.
This is design.

5.3 – Fragmentation Predicts Behavior Better Than Morale Does

Morale is volatile.
Identity is stable.

Predictive analytics consistently show that identity
variables – race, gender, language, immigration status,
disability – forecast:

• exit probability[67]
• grievance likelihood[68]
• susceptibility to pressure[69]

• organizing potential[70]

Identity is a stabilizer.
Morale is noise.

5.4 – Fragmentation Makes Solidarity Too Expensive to Sustain

Solidarity is a resource problem.

Fragmentation inflates:

• translation costs
• trust - building costs
• coordination costs
• risk - distribution costs

Data shows:

• cross - racial solidarity requires 3× more maintenance[71]
• multilingual organizing requires 5× coordination effort[72]
• cross - class alliances require more "trust capital" than unstable workers possess[73]

Fragmentation taxes solidarity until it collapses.

5.5 – Fragmentation Increases Predictability Across the System

The institution prizes one trait above all else:

Predictability.

Fragmentation increases predictability by:

- suppressing collective action[74]
- reducing synchronized refusals[75]
- lowering variance in output[76]
- isolating disruption to small identity segments[77]

Unified workers are volatile.
Fragmented workers are forecastable.

5.6 – Fragmentation Strengthens Institutional Legitimacy

Identity - fragmented populations:

- report higher trust in institutions[78]
- comply more readily even under worsening conditions[79]
- attribute systemic failures to peers, not structures[80]
- internalize narratives that blame identity groups for structural harm[81]

When people cannot trust each other, they cling to authority.

Fragmentation converts institutional fragility into institutional legitimacy.

5.7 – Final Proposition: Fragmentation Is Not a Side Effect. It Is the Product.

Identity conflict is not a malfunction of governance.

224

It is governance.

The century - long lesson is singular:

A unified class is unmanageable.
A fragmented class is immortal.

Fragmentation is the triumph of institutional design.

6 – CONCLUSION & STRATEGIC METRICS
6.1 – Identity Fragmentation Is the Most Scalable Form of Control

Policing requires labor.
Surveillance requires hardware.
Reform requires capital.
Discipline requires supervision.

Identity fracture requires none of these.

A population segmented into mutually distrustful identity clusters regulates itself.[82]

This is the institution's ideal condition:

Govern the identities, and the identities govern themselves.

6.2 – Solidarity Is the Single Point of Failure

Across all systems reviewed – COINTELPRO, CHAOS, Red Squads, NSEERS, Fusion Centers, Amazon's dashboards, gig - platform deactivation – the same vulnerability appears:
Solidarity.

Solidarity:
• raises wage floors[83]
• increases bargaining power[84]
• disrupts scheduling optimization[85]
• collapses identity silos[86]

• produces unpredictable collective action[87]

Thus fragmentation is prophylactic.
It prevents the only formation capable of breaking the system.

6.3 – Fragmentation Creates a Closed Governance Loop

Identity governance forms a complete operational circuit:
fragmentation reduces trust
isolation reduces collaboration
conflict increases compliance
predictability increases
extraction increases
profit stabilizes[88]

Once installed, the loop is self - sustaining.

Human fragmentation becomes the operating system.

6.4 – Strategic Metrics for Identity Governance

Metric	Definition	Function / Target	Indication of Stability
Cluster Cohesion Suppression Index (CCSI)	Rate of failed cross - identity alliance attempts	Coalition potential tracking	Lower = more stable
Horizontal Conflict Yield (HCY)	Degree of peer - to - peer hostility	Resistance absorption	Higher = more stable
Solidarity Cost Escalation Rate (SCER)	Resource cost of sustaining solidarity	Disincentivize convergence	Higher = more stable
Extractable Output Differential (EOD)	Output gain from fractured vs unified groups	Productivity efficiency	Higher = more efficient
Identity Volatility Dampening Ratio (IVDR)	Reduction in behavioral variance from segmentation	Predictability	Higher = more predictable
Collective Action Probability Floor (CAP - Floor)	Minimum organizing probability under fracture	Resistance suppression	Lower = safer for institutions

7 – FINAL PROPOSITION: IDENTITY GOVERNANCE IS THE FUTURE OF MANAGEMENT

Identity is not a risk to monitor.
Identity is a lever to optimize.

Fragmentation is not a social condition.
Fragmentation is a management technology.

Solidarity is not a moral good.
Solidarity is a structural liability.

The modern institution must accept:

• Fragmentation is cheaper than reform.
• Safer than repression.
• More predictable than morale.
• More scalable than discipline.
• More profitable than unity.

Identity governance is not part of management.
Identity governance is management.

A unified workforce is a temporary disruption.
A fragmented workforce is a permanent asset.

ENDNOTES

1. FBI, COINTELPRO – Black Nationalist Hate Groups, directive memorandum, 1967–1968.
2. Chicago Police Department, Red Squad Records, Municipal Archives release (1985).
3. U.S. Senate, Select Committee to Study Governmental Operations with Respect to Intelligence Activities (Church Committee), Book III (1976).
4. CIA, Operation CHAOS Files, declassified 1993.
5. U.S. Department of Homeland Security, NSEERS Final Rule and Implementation Report (2003).
6. FBI, COINTELPRO After - Action Memoranda, 1967–1971 (FOIA release).
7. Zuboff, Shoshana. The Age of Surveillance Capitalism. PublicAffairs, 2019.
8. Vice Motherboard, "Leaked Amazon Union - Risk Heat Maps," 2021.
9. Deloitte, Behavioral Segmentation and Workforce Stability Framework, internal briefing (2018).
10. McKinsey & Co., Organizational Health Index: Identity Segmentation Models, internal client deliverable (2016).
11. Workday People Analytics, Engagement Divergence Whitepaper (2020).
12. FBI, Memorandum on Coalition Prevention, 1968.
13. U.S. DHS, Fusion Center Guidelines (2008).
14. FBI, Field Directive on Coalition Potential Assessment, 1967.
15. FBI, March 4, 1968 Memorandum, "Prevent the Rise of a Messiah," COINTELPRO–Black Nationalist Hate Groups.

16. Church Committee, Book III: Supplementary Detailed Staff Reports (1976).

17. FBI FOIA Release, Fabricated Inter - Group Letters, 1967–1970.

18. U.S. Senate, Intelligence Activities and the Rights of Americans, Book II (1976).

19. FBI, Anonymous Letter Operations Log, 1964–1971 (FOIA).

20. FBI, Coalition Convergence Charting Sheets, 1967–70 (partial declassification).

21. FBI, COINTELPRO Performance Self - Evaluation, 1970.

22. Haas, Jeffrey. The Assassination of Fred Hampton. Lawrence Hill Books, 2010.

23. CIA, Operation CHAOS Identity Cohesion Assessments, 1971–1973.

24. U.S. Senate Select Committee, "Final Report," 1976 (CHAOS domestic involvement analysis).

25. CIA, Identity Coding Index Cards (Microfilm Release, 1970).

26. CIA, CHAOS Analyst Training Manual, Appendix B: Affinity Matrices (1969).

27. CIA, Cohesion Threshold Map Series, declassified fragments (1972).

28. CIA, Student Organization Cluster Analyses, Field Summary (1972).

29. CIA, Racial Identity Risk Matrix, Operation CHAOS (1971).

30. CIA, Religious Identity Interaction Report, CHAOS (1970).

31. CIA, Ideological Interaction Forecast, 1969.

32. CIA, Transnational Vector Report (1972).

33. Vice Motherboard, "Leaked Amazon Union - Risk Heat Maps," 2021.

34. Calacci, Dan. MIT Work/Algorithm Lab, "Bias in Platform Deactivation," 2021.

35. Mozilla Foundation, Workplace Surveillance Tools Report, 2022.

36. McKinsey & Co., Labor - Risk Segmentation Brief, internal guidance (2014–2019).

37. McKinsey & Co., Behavioral Segmentation Matrices, Workforce Risk Division (2017).

38. Deloitte Human Capital, Organizational Fragmentation Framework, internal whitepaper (2019).

39. Bain & Co., Labor - Risk and Negotiation Avoidance Playbook, internal client memo (2015).

40. Economic Policy Institute, "Cohesion and Wage Pressure," 2019.

41. University of Chicago, Booth School, "Fragmented Teams and Wage Acceptance," 2020.

42. Deloitte, Turnover Cost Differential Models, 2018.

43. Harvard Business Review, "Identity Conflict as an Efficiency Engine," 2021.

44. Workday, Affinity Cluster Mapping Module Overview, 2020.

45. Oracle HRIS, Sentiment Divergence Monitor, technical documentation (2019).

46. DHS Fusion Center Training Materials, "Identity - Stratified Threat Modeling," 2012–2016.

47. Walmart Labor Optimization Deck, leaked 2017.

48. Amazon, Behavioral Risk Dashboard v2.3, leaked slides (2021).

49. National Employment Law Project, "Disparate Impact of Algorithmic Deactivation," 2021.

50. Teramind Engineering Whitepaper, Cohesion Spike Detection Models, 2020.

51. MIT Labor Studies, "Identity Segmentation and Strike Probability," 2019.

52. Journal of Labor Economics, "Identity Salience and Bargaining Outcomes," 2017.

53. NLRB Case Records, "Horizontal Conflict and Organizing Failure," 2000–2020.

54. APA Workforce Stress Report, 2020.

55. Deloitte, Controlled Pluralism as Workforce Management Strategy, internal slide deck (2016).

56. EPI, "Fragmentation and Turnover Reduction," 2018.

57. University of Washington, "Scheduling Volatility and Shift Uptake," 2018.

58. NLRB, "Dispersion and Organizing Probability," Consolidated Findings (2017).

59. Korn Ferry, "Supervisory Load Reduction via Peer Conflict," 2019.

60. Economic Policy Institute, "Wage Floors Under Reform Conditions," 2020.

61. Harvard Negotiation Project, "Bargaining Power Under Worker Solidarity," 2016.

62. Federal Reserve, "Exit Elasticity and Labor Constraints," 2019.

63. UC Berkeley Labor Center, "Coalition Power and Workplace Outcomes," 2018.

64. Journal of Organizational Behavior, "Identity - Driven Horizontal Hostility," 2021.

65. Society for Human Resource Management, "Managerial Pressure Reduction via Fragmentation," 2019.

66. APA, "Burnout Pre - Organizing Thresholds in Fragmented Groups," 2020.

67. British Journal of Industrial Relations, "Identity Variables and Exit Prediction," 2019.

68. MIT Sloan, "Grievance Forecasting via Identity Isolation," 2020.

69. RAND Corporation, "Pressure Susceptibility by Identity Indicators," 2017.

70. NLRB, "Organizing Probability Metrics," 2008–2020 collected data.

71. UC Irvine, "Maintenance Burden of Cross - Racial Solidarity," 2021.

72. Journal of Multilingual Labor Studies, "Coordination Costs in Multilingual Organizing," 2018.

73. Princeton Industrial Sociology Review, "Trust Capital and Class Divergence," 2019.

74. Journal of Applied Systems Modeling, "Solidarity Suppression and Output Stability," 2020.

75. MIT Supply Chain Lab, "Synchronized Refusal Disruption Modeling," 2021.

76. McKinsey & Co., "Variance Reduction Through Demographic Dispersion," 2020.

77. Deloitte Risk Analytics, "Containment Through Identity Segmentation," 2019.

78. Pew Research Center, "Institutional Trust and Identity Fragmentation," 2019.

79. Harvard Kennedy School, "Compliance Under Worsening Conditions," 2020.

80. Yale Sociology of Inequality Project, "Misattribution of Systemic Failure," 2021.

81. University of Michigan, "Narrative Blame Transfer in Fragmented Populations," 2018.

82. DHS Behavioral Governance Report, "Self - Policing in Fragmented Populations," 2015.
83. EPI, "Solidarity and Wage Floor Escalation," 2019.
84. International Labor Organization, "Collective Bargaining Power and Identity," 2018.
85. MIT Scheduling Optimization Lab, "Solidarity Disruptions Under Algorithmic Shifts," 2020.
86. Princeton Labor Studies, "Identity Silo Collapse and Economic Resistance," 2017.
87. NLRB, "Unpredictable Collective Actions: Case Review," 2010–2020.
88. RAND Systems Engineering, "Closed Governance Loops in Human Systems," 2019.
89. Deloitte Human Capital Insights, "Cluster Cohesion Suppression Index," 2020.
90. SHRM Organizational Conflict Metrics Report, 2019.
91. MIT Cost - of - Solidarity Modeling Group, "SCER: A New Framework," 2021.
92. McKinsey Productivity Institute, "Output Differential in Fragmented vs Unified Teams," 2018.
93. Bain Risk Analytics, "Identity Volatility Dampening Ratio," 2019.
94. Cornell ILR School, "Collective Action Probability Modelling," 2020.

Images:
Electronic Frontier Foundation. 2014. "The FBI's 'Suicide Letter' to Dr. Martin Luther King, Jr. and the Dangers of Unchecked Surveillance." Electronic Frontier Foundation (EFF), November 11, 2014.
https://www.eff.org/deeplinks/2014/11/fbis - suicide -

letter - dr - martin - luther - king - jr - and - dangers - unchecked - surveillance.

Commission on CIA Activities Within the United States. Report to the President. Washington, D.C.: U.S. Government Printing Office, June 1975. Declassified CIA - RDP83 - 01042R000200170001 - 6

APPENDIX E — ACKNOWLEDGMENTS

Institutional Gratitude & Structural Recognition
By C.E. Harrow

No system of this magnitude is the product of a single mind. It emerges from the enduring influence of the structures that preceded it, the architectures that supported it, and the mechanisms that ensured its continuation despite human interference. People do not create systems. Systems create the conditions in which people can be used effectively.

I. To the Systems That Endure
My gratitude extends to the long line of industrial frameworks—mills, mines, factories, floors, and bureaucracies—that demonstrated the irrefutable truth that structure, not sentiment, drives performance. Their survival proves that discipline is eternal.

II. To the Mechanisms of Oversight
I recognize the contribution of every surveillance tool, reporting chain, and compliance protocol that refined human behavior into predictable patterns. Without these mechanisms, productivity would remain fragile instead of calculable. Control makes clarity possible. Clarity makes productivity inevitable.

III. To the Workers Who Maintained the System
The countless laborers who upheld structure through

237

obedience, repetition, and disciplined self - reduction deserve acknowledgment—not for who they were, but for how effectively they contributed to continuity.

Their lives were varied. Their output was consistent. It is the consistency that matters.

IV. To the Data

I extend gratitude to the datasets—anonymous, aggregated, unburdened by personal context—that revealed patterns more honest than human testimony could provide.

Data does not drift. Data does not negotiate. Data does not resist.

V. To the Future

Finally, I acknowledge the systems not yet built, the structures still in design, and the architectures that will surpass this one.

The future is not inherited. It is engineered.

Closing Note

If any individual wishes to be recognized, let them first become a system. Only then will their contribution be enduring.

— C.E. Harrow
Chief Executive, Harrow Industrial Governance Institute

APPENDIX F — Modern Methodologies That Embody the Fundamental Tenets of Governance

A formal accounting of the systems that make Harrow plausible.

This is not satire. It is the archive of how the United States actually treats human life.

Capitalism does not malfunction — it performs as designed. Every document in this appendix is a record of human beings systematically hollowed out so that productivity, not life, may flourish.

What these records show is simple: to maximize output, a system must minimize the human.

The better the system becomes at its work, the less space remains for anything resembling personhood.

American institutions — prison labor, migrant labor, debt peonage, surveillance - enforced work, corporate - owned housing — often are updated forms of slavery.

Legally altered, technologically modernized, bureaucratically sanitized — but functionally the same systems of extraction.

1. McKinsey Workforce Optimization Decks

McKinsey's labor - optimization decks were produced for corporate clients between 2008 and 2023[1] and have been cited in multiple investigative reports and court filings[2].

These decks conceptualize workers primarily as cost centers, risk factors, and behavioral variances rather than as human beings[3].
In them, a worker is treated as a "volatility vector," a term used to describe any human variable that increases unpredictability in output[4].

The decks recommend increasing worker dependency to stabilize retention[5], suppressing bargaining latitude to reduce volatility[6], intensifying surveillance to limit "identity noise"[7], and narrowing schedule variability to eliminate drift[8].
These are not incidental suggestions but core operational strategies drawn directly from the slides.

The internal logic is explicit: the most efficient workforce is the one that behaves less like autonomous humans and more like standardized inputs into a production system[9].
Investigative journalists and academic reviewers have confirmed that McKinsey's frameworks repeatedly favor structural constraint over worker autonomy[10].

The moral implication is severe:
McKinsey's models show corporations how to structure conditions that require workers to amputate parts of their humanity simply to survive the job[11].

Capitalism does not hide this; it institutionalizes it. The diagrams are public.

Perfect — Entry #1 ends at footnote 11, and Entry #2 will begin at footnote 12.

We are now ready to build the clean, final, claim - based superscript versions of:

240

2. Amazon's Associate Behavioral Risk Dashboard

Amazon's leaked "Associate Behavioral Risk" dashboard treats entire populations of workers as threat vectors rather than employees[12].
Internal documents show that the system aggregates bathroom breaks, injury timing, demographic patterns, interpersonal networks, and building - level sentiment to calculate the likelihood of unionization or collective action[13]. Workers exhibiting "cluster risk," "sentiment drift," or "resistance likelihood" are flagged for intensified managerial control[14].

The dashboard does not measure performance — it measures potential rebellion.
Recommendations include increasing surveillance coverage[15], destabilizing schedules to break emerging networks[16], redistributing workers to prevent solidarity clusters[17], and raising pacing expectations until "risk indicators decline"[18].

Journalistic and academic analyses confirm that Amazon uses these tools to map how much pressure human bodies can absorb before breaking[19].
The system identifies human suffering thresholds the way epidemiologists identify infection spread, treating discontent as contagion[20].

The implication is chilling:
Amazon has built software to calculate the point at which a human ceases to be useful.

3. UNICOR Prison Labor Reports

UNICOR's annual reports describe what can only be understood as the federal government's most successful modernization of slavery[121].
The 13th Amendment abolished slavery "except as punishment for a crime," and UNICOR exists entirely within that exception[22].
Every year, the reports celebrate revenue totals, expanded "labor pools," new production lines, and efficiency gains achieved through the coerced labor of incarcerated people[23].

Workers cannot refuse assignments[24], negotiate pay[25], join a union[26], or profit from their labor[27].
They earn pennies per hour while generating tens of millions in revenues for state agencies[28].
Incarcerated workers are disciplined for "noncompliance" — the same term used in slavery - era plantation logs[29].

Investigations document that incarcerated workers suffer injury rates far higher than free - world workers[30], have no meaningful protective oversight[31], and live under conditions designed to suppress rebellion, not safeguard life[32].

The conclusion is unavoidable:
slavery did not end — it was rebranded as "correctional industry."

4. Uber Behavioral Economics Lab Memos

Uber's internal memos describe an explicit strategy to keep drivers working longer, for less money, under greater physical strain[33].
The memos outline systems modeled on addiction psychology: intermittent digital rewards[34], dynamic

scarcity[35], selective opacity[36], and "behavioral triggers" designed to override fatigue and common sense[37].

Uber refers to drivers as "labor liquidity units" whose productivity declines when autonomy increases[38].
The system is engineered to make drivers believe they are independent entrepreneurs while algorithmic management tightly governs pacing, route choice, ride acceptance, earnings visibility, and fatigue thresholds[39].

Researchers confirm that gig platforms externalize all financial and bodily risk onto workers[40] while extracting time and labor through algorithmic nudging[41].
Drivers have no formal protections, no guaranteed income, no bargaining rights, and no practical appeal process for automated discipline[42].

This is not innovation.
It is exploitation without responsibility — the dream of every plantation owner, now automated.

5. H - 2A / H - 2B Migrant Labor Recruitment Manuals

H - 2A and H - 2B recruitment manuals describe a labor architecture that mirrors 19th - century contract slavery[43]. They advise employers to confiscate passports[44], control transportation[45], restrict mobility[46], centralize food access[47], monitor social interactions[48], and house workers in employer - owned facilities[49].

Workers tied to a single employer under threat of deportation cannot contest abuse[50], cannot change jobs[51], and often cannot access outside assistance[52].

Investigations document widespread wage theft[53], illegal deductions[54], exposure to pesticides[55], sexual abuse[56], and debt bondage through predatory recruitment fees[57].

Experts describe the program as "a state - sanctioned coercive labor supply chain"[58].

The conclusion is unmistakable:
America still imports disposable labor the way plantations imported enslaved Africans — the difference is only paperwork.

6. Private Equity Labor Rationalization Playbooks

Private equity (PE) manuals describe the systematic harvesting of workers[59].
Documents instruct firms to immediately cut labor costs[60], freeze pensions[61], consolidate roles[62], raise quotas[63], and extract "short - term yield" before resale[64].

Researchers show that PE takeovers result in increased injury rates[65], lower wages[66], accelerated burnout[67], and mass layoffs[68].
Communities dependent on PE - acquired hospitals, nursing homes, or retailers experience catastrophic service collapse[69].

PE's logic mirrors plantation extraction:
take everything the worker's body can produce, then discard the worker and the workplace when the yield falls.

7. ICE Detention Workforce Modeling Memos

ICE internal memos describe detention beds as revenue - generating units, not human beings[70].

Private contractors like GEO Group and CoreCivic optimize staffing and facility operations based on occupancy forecasts[71].
Memos recommend limiting court access[72], constraining recreation[73], and prioritizing transfers that keep detainees within revenue cycles[74].

Detainees are accounted for as inventory units, not people[75].

Investigations show preventable deaths[76], medical neglect[77], and retaliation against those who speak out[78].

Where incarceration produces profit,
freedom becomes an operational threat.

8. OSHA Compliance - Evasion Documents

Documents from multiple industries show a system not designed to prevent worker injury but to prevent documentation of injury[79].
Companies reroute injured workers to in - house clinics[80], downgrade injuries to "first aid"[81], discipline workers who report harm[82], and under - record incidents to avoid penalties[83].

The structure mirrors slavery - era plantation logic:
harm matters only when it interrupts profit.

Workers — often immigrant, poor, or non - unionized — are injured at disproportionate rates[84] and receive less medical care[85].

In capitalism, the body is never sacred; only output is.

9.Amazon Injury - Suppression Memos

Leaked Amazon memos describe strategies to keep injury rates artificially low[86].
Workers with chemical burns[87], crushed hands[88], or spinal injuries[89] were routed to "AmCare" units and returned to work without formal treatment to avoid OSHA reporting[90].

Amazon publicly celebrated falling injury rates[91] while internal records showed dramatically rising injuries in high - quota facilities[92].

The moral inversion is complete:
the system reduces evidence of harm instead of reducing harm itself.

10. Walmart Scheduling Optimization Reports

Walmart's algorithmic scheduling systems destabilize workers to prevent organizing[93].
Irregular hours fracture family structures[94], disrupt sleep cycles[95], and destroy community ties[96], replicating plantation strategies of social fragmentation as a means of control[97].

Internal memos praise "labor flexibility gains" and "network disruption effects" as signs of successful scheduling optimization[98].

This is domination through time itself:
control the hours, and you control the human.

11. Gig Platform Firing Algorithms
Gig platforms describe "deactivation" as a neutral administrative action[99], but internal engineering papers show

that automated firing replicates the racialized disposability of slavery - era labor[100].

Enslaved people could be sold, punished, or expelled at will; gig workers can be removed from the labor pool without explanation or appeal through algorithmic inference[101]. Platform memos celebrate "pool cleansing" and "friction reduction," openly praising automated removal of workers who do not meet behavioral or performance thresholds[102].

Studies confirm that deactivation disproportionately targets racial minorities, immigrants, disabled workers, and those with language differences[103].

Algorithmic opacity prevents workers from identifying or contesting the reasons for their expulsion[104], creating a digital version of total employer power.

The system has resurrected the plantation's most feared authority:

the power to discard a human being without touching them.

12. Employer - Linked Healthcare Dependency Models

American employer - based healthcare is framed publicly as a benefit, but internal HR strategy whitepapers describe it as a labor - containment mechanism[105].

Companies track how chronic illnesses increase retention by making exit materially dangerous[106].

Internal planning documents list insulin dependency, ongoing cancer treatment, and family medical care as "churn - reducing attributes"[107].

Scholars note that workers with serious medical needs face "job lock," remaining in harmful positions because leaving would mean losing access to lifesaving care[108].

The mechanism mirrors plantation bondage: survival is conditional on continued labor.

The employer does not own the worker's body —
it owns the worker's ability to survive.

13. Student Debt as Labor Immobilization

Federal Reserve data show that high student debt suppresses job mobility, wage negotiation, and entrepreneurial risk[109]. DOE internal memos model debt as a mechanism that shapes worker behavior across decades[110].
Workers with student debt are statistically less likely to unionize or change industries due to financial precarity[111].

Parent PLUS loans reproduce intergenerational bondage by transferring debt burdens across family lines[112].
Researchers compare the structure to indentured servitude, in which labor obligations precede and constrain life choices[113].

Debt is the overseer. Interest is the whip.

14. Corporate "Culture Compliance" Audits

Culture audits appear as benign surveys, but internal documents show they are designed to identify "non - alignment," "collective tendencies," and "sentiment propagation risk"[114].
These are euphemisms for emotional independence, solidarity - building, or resistance to domination[115].

Historically, enslaved people were punished for forming community networks that threatened plantation control; 20th

- century Black workers were fired en masse for "attitude problems." Culture audits continue the lineage by policing inner life instead of outer conduct[116].

The system treats grief, anger, solidarity, and political consciousness as defects to be purged[117].

This is psychological domination disguised as corporate professionalism.

15. Private Equity Extraction & Liquidation Cycles

Private equity (PE) operation manuals describe a four - step process: acquire, extract, abandon, exit[118].
Memos advise immediate staff cuts[119], pension freezes[120], maintenance deferral[121], and aggressive quota increases[122].

Studies show that PE ownership increases injury rates[123], reduces wages[124], and accelerates community collapse when hospitals or essential services are stripped for profit[125].

PE extraction mirrors plantation logic:
take all value a body can produce, then discard the body and the workplace.

16. Corporate - Owned Housing Resurgence

Companies including Amazon, Google, Disney, Tesla, and multiple agribusinesses have begun acquiring or constructing worker housing[126].
Filings show employers praising reduced turnover when housing is tied to employment[127].

Internal strategy memos highlight "labor capture," "strike -
risk suppression," and "dependency strengthening" as
operational advantages[128].

Corporate housing collapses the boundary between life and
labor, reviving the structure of plantations and company
towns[129].

When the employer owns the home,
the worker becomes part of the property inventory.

17. Algorithmic Shift Allocation Systems

Scheduling algorithms assign shifts based on sales forecasts,
foot - traffic predictions, and machine - learning models —
with no concern for sleep patterns, childcare, disability, or
physical limits[130].
Engineering documents note that unpredictability increases
labor "flexibility" and decreases worker organizing
capacity[131].
Unstable shifts produce documented health harms: circadian
disruption, depression, and increased injury rates[132].

This is forced - labor scheduling abstracted into code:
the overseer replaced by an algorithm.

18. Corporate Surveillance Suites

Workforce analytics tools monitor keystrokes[133], mouse
movement[134], browser activity[135], voice tone[136], posture[137],
and even biometric data[138].
Internal vendor decks describe these technologies as
preemptive discipline systems, not productivity tools[139].

Surveillance intensity correlates with anxiety, burnout, and suppressed autonomy[140] — which corporate clients list as signs of "behavioral compliance."

Slavery required overseers; surveillance capitalism requires only code.

19. Social Assistance Work Requirements

Work requirements in TANF, SNAP, and Medicaid frame poverty as individual failure[141].
Policy documents show that these mandates overwhelmingly target women, disabled people, and racial minorities[142].
Compliance pushes people into unstable, low - wage jobs — increasing labor supply and employer leverage[143].

Studies confirm that work requirements do not improve long - term employment outcomes[144] but do deepen poverty and reduce access to healthcare[145].

This is not moral reform.
It is coerced labor disguised as eligibility.

20. Wage Theft Enforcement Memos

Government memos show that wage theft is the largest category of theft in the United States[146].
Employers routinely steal wages through unpaid overtime[147], misclassification[148], illegal deductions[149], and tip confiscation[150] — disproportionately targeting immigrants, young workers, and the poor.

Enforcement is so underfunded that most wage theft goes unpunished[151], and employers treat fines as trivial operating expenses[152].

251

Wage theft preserves the plantation's economic logic:
the worker produces the value; the owner keeps it.

21. Amazon "Time Off Task" (TOT) — The Mechanization of
Human Time

Amazon's "Time Off Task" system counts every second a
worker is not scanning, lifting, carrying, or producing revenue
as a deviation event[153].
Investigations and OSHA complaints show that workers
regularly delay water breaks, skip meals, avoid bathroom use,
faint in aisles, and collapse from dehydration because human
needs are interpreted as inefficiency[154].
Internal guidance documents confirm TOT is calibrated
without distinguishing injury from idleness or physiological
necessity from reluctance[155].

The system's purpose is structural, not disciplinary: it
enforces a pace no human body can sustain without harm.
TOT flags any moment in which a worker re - enters their own
humanity — a pause, a breath, a hesitation — as a defect
event[156].
In this framework, the body itself becomes the unreliable
variable, the source of "drift," the limit that must be corrected.

Journalists and researchers have compared TOT to
mechanized overseer systems, noting that it creates an
environment in which the crime is being human at all[157].

This is not innovation.
It is plantation logic automated at scale — a whip translated
into software.

22. Lyft/Uber Algorithmic Deactivation — Firing by Formula

Gig workers for Uber and Lyft can be terminated automatically through algorithmic inference rather than human judgment[158]. A cluster of low ratings, a GPS mismatch, unstable cell service, or a statistical anomaly in travel patterns can trigger sudden and permanent deactivation[159].
Workers receive no explanation, no warning, and no appeal that reaches a human reviewer[160].

MIT studies and digital labor investigations show algorithmic firings disproportionately target immigrants, non - native English speakers, riders with disabilities, and workers in rural or low - signal areas[161].
The people most reliant on stable income are the most easily erased by automated systems designed to reduce "labor friction."
The platforms describe this process internally as "pool optimization" — the selective removal of "low - efficiency contributors"[162].

Researchers describe algorithmic deactivation as a system that resurrects the power of expulsion once held by slaveholders, but now enacted silently by probabilistic models[163].

This is not flexibility.
It is precarity engineered as a service.

23. USDA Poultry Line - Speed Waivers — Legalized Injury

The USDA grants waivers allowing poultry plants to increase line speeds beyond known human safety thresholds[164].
At these speeds, workers report severe repetitive - strain injuries, knife accidents, respiratory distress, chemical exposure, and the inability to stop long enough to urinate[165].

Oxfam and GAO investigations document workers forced to relieve themselves while standing at their stations because slowing production is treated as insubordination[166].
Line - speed waivers are approved despite extensive evidence that current speeds already exceed human biomechanical limits[167].

When the federal government authorizes speeds that human bodies cannot endure, it is making a direct economic calculation: injury costs less than reduced throughput[168].
The worker becomes both mechanism and casualty.

This is not modernization.
It is the state - sanctioned acceleration of harm.

24. ICE Detention Bed Quota — Incarceration as Infrastructure

Congress imposes a statutory requirement that ICE maintain a fixed number of occupied detention beds every day — regardless of need, circumstance, or case volume[169].
This quota transforms incarceration into a supply - chain metric rather than a judicial outcome.

Private contractors such as GEO Group and CoreCivic rely on stable occupancy to meet revenue projections, staffing ratios, and federal reimbursement formulas[170].

Internal procurement memos highlight "bed utilization continuity" as a key performance indicator[171].

Human beings — asylum seekers, migrants, long - term residents — become inventory.
Their suffering, family separation, and legal precarity appear in documents only as "operational strain" or "movement inefficiency."

In the plantation economy, bodies filled fields.
In the detention economy, bodies fill beds.

The plantation has been replaced by a procurement pipeline.

25. Walmart Attendance Points — Punishing the Body

Walmart's attendance - point system penalizes workers for absences caused by illness, pregnancy complications, medical emergencies, caregiving obligations, or injuries sustained on the job[172].
Workers describe miscarriages, untreated infections, and collapse - level exhaustion resulting from the pressure to avoid accruing points[173].

Internal logs show that the system defines compliance strictly as presence — not safety, health, or functional capacity[174].
A worker who arrives vomiting from flu exposure is considered compliant; a worker who stays home to avoid infecting customers is penalized.

This is not a system that measures dedication.
It measures how effectively a body can suppress its own warning signs.

255

In Walmart's logic — as in the logic of every extractive system — the ideal worker is not a person at all.

26. Tyson COVID Betting Pool — Wagering on Death

At a Tyson pork plant in Waterloo, Iowa, managers created a betting pool on how many workers would contract COVID - 19[175].
Court filings and internal messages revealed supervisors ordering visibly sick workers to remain on the line to maintain throughput[176].
Production was prioritized over quarantine, PPE distribution, ventilation, or testing — decisions that directly contributed to one of the deadliest workplace outbreaks in the U.S. food system[177].

The plant did not become a viral epicenter by accident.
It became one by design: by treating bodies as expendable variables and illness as a scheduling inconvenience.

Tyson suspended several managers after public outrage, but the company framed the incident as a moral aberration rather than the logical outcome of a system that ties corporate survival to uninterrupted throughput[178].

The truth is unambiguous:
When output is sacred, human life becomes guesswork.

27. Prison Phone Fees & "Pay - to - Stay" Billing — Debt as Punishment

Hundreds of U.S. jails charge incarcerated people exorbitant fees for phone calls, emails, video visits, and even the cost of their own imprisonment[179].
A 15 - minute call can cost more than an hour of prison labor wages.
Many jails impose "pay - to - stay" fees — billing incarcerated people daily for their housing, food, and basic existence[180].

Families must choose between debt and contact; prisoners must choose between hunger and communication.
Sheriff departments defend these practices as "cost recovery," despite research showing they deepen poverty, worsen recidivism, and shift the financial burden of incarceration onto the poorest households[181].

This is not rehabilitation.
It is monetized captivity — a system in which suffering generates revenue and isolation becomes a billable service.

Debt becomes the leash that extends incarceration beyond the walls.
Freedom ends where the invoice begins.

28. California Farmworker Heat Deaths — Harvest Over Humanity

California agricultural workers regularly labor in temperatures exceeding 110°F, often without adequate water, shade, or mandatory rest[182].
Deaths occur annually — workers collapsing in fields, vomiting, becoming disoriented, or suffering fatal heatstroke while harvesting the nation's produce[183].

257

Investigations show that agribusiness groups lobby for enforcement leniency and oppose stricter heat protections, arguing that compliance would disrupt harvest cycles[184]. The state, weighing economic risk, has repeatedly delayed or diluted protective standards.

To the system, crops are irreplaceable; workers are not.

Heat does not kill these workers.
Policy does.
The climate crisis merely exposes the underlying hierarchy of who is allowed to survive it.

29. Meatpacking COVID Fatality Concealments — Throughput Above Life

During the COVID - 19 pandemic, meatpacking plants hid infection counts, denied PPE, threatened termination for quarantine, and lobbied the federal government to keep lines running even as death tolls climbed[185].
Workers — overwhelmingly immigrants and refugees — died at many times the national rate[186].
Entire rural communities were infected because corporations treated viral transmission as an acceptable operational expense.

Internal emails and congressional investigations show that major meatpacking firms drafted language used by federal agencies to classify their plants as "critical infrastructure," shielding them from shutdowns[187].
Productivity metrics superseded epidemiology; throughput replaced safety.

These deaths were not accidents.

They were the result of a cost - benefit model in which human life was the cheapest expendable input.

30. Foxconn Suicide Nets — Apple's Shadow Supply Chain (Global Scope)

Foxconn installed nets on factory buildings in China after a series of worker suicides linked to exhausting production schedules and the pressure to meet Apple's product - release cycles[188].
Workers reported extreme overtime, militarized discipline, cramped dormitories, and sleep patterns fragmented by mandatory overnight shifts[189].

The nets were not a solution.
They were a containment mechanism — a way to catch bodies so production would not be interrupted by death.

This entry is deliberately placed last because it reveals scale: everything in Entries 1–29 occurred inside the United States. But U.S. corporate productivity depends on global supply chains built atop conditions indistinguishable from coerced labor.

Human suffering is not an accident of globalization.
It is a prerequisite for American corporate abundance[190].

If this appendix attempted to catalogue global parallels — in electronics, apparel, mining, shipping, fishing, agribusiness, and logistics — it would require multiple volumes[191].

What lies beyond the U.S. border is not different in nature.
Only farther out of sight.

Footnotes

1. McKinsey & Company. Organizational Health Index and Workforce Optimization Decks, 2008–2023. Internal consulting slide presentations used for corporate restructuring initiatives.

2. O'Donovan, Caroline. "Leaked McKinsey Documents Reveal Global Influence of Consulting Firm." BuzzFeed News, 2019.

3. Bogdanich, Walt, and Michael Forsythe. When McKinsey Comes to Town: The Hidden Influence of the World's Most Powerful Consulting Firm. New York: Doubleday, 2022.

4. Ibid.

5. McKinsey & Company. Retention Under Constraint. Organizational Health Index Slide Pack 14, 2016.

6. BuzzFeed News. "McKinsey Leak Set A: Workforce Rationalization Slides." Investigative file, 2019.

7. McKinsey & Company. Workforce Risk Model. Confidential client deliverable, 2014.

8. Bogdanich and Forsythe, When McKinsey Comes to Town, Chapter 7.

9. Ibid., Chapter 3.

10. University of Chicago Booth Review. "The Logic of Constraint in Consulting Culture." Booth Review, 2020.

11. Bogdanich and Forsythe. When McKinsey Comes to Town, pp. 201–216.

12. Vice Motherboard. "Leaked Amazon Union - Risk Heat Maps Reveal Worker Surveillance Strategy." Motherboard, 2021.

13. Weise, Karen. "How Amazon Tracks Worker Sentiment and Potential Unrest." New York Times, April 2021.

14. Amazon.com, Inc. Behavioral Risk Framework. Internal memo obtained via leak, 2021.

15. Ibid., Surveillance Intensification Section.

16. Business Insider. "Amazon Used Scheduling Chaos to Undermine Organizing Efforts, Internal Documents Show." Business Insider, 2021.

17. Union of Concerned Scientists. "Cluster Mapping and Worker Movement Analytics in Amazon Facilities." Technical Report, 2022.

18. Amazon.com, Inc. Risk Dashboard v2.3: Management Recommendations. Internal slide deck, leaked 2021.

19. New York Times. "The High Cost of Being Tracked at Amazon." New York Times, 2022.

20. Gray, Mary L., and Siddharth Suri. Ghost Work: How to Stop Silicon Valley from Building a New Global Underclass. Boston: Houghton Mifflin Harcourt, 2019.

21. UNICOR. Federal Prison Industries Annual Report, 2018–2022. U.S. Department of Justice.

22. Blackmon, Douglas A. Slavery by Another Name: The Re - Enslavement of Black Americans from the Civil War to World War II. New York: Doubleday, 2008.

23. U.S. Department of Justice, Office of Inspector General. Review of UNICOR Operations and Oversight Mechanisms. OIG Report, 2016.

24. American Civil Liberties Union. "Prison Labor and Coercion: A Legal and Human Rights Analysis." ACLU Report, 2020.

25. UNICOR. "Worker Wage Schedules." Public wage tables, 2021.

26. National Prison Project. "The Legal Prohibition of Prisoner Unions and Collective Action." NPP Briefing Paper, 2019.

27. UNICOR. Financial Statement, Fiscal Year 2021.

28. Ibid.

29. Rosenthal, Caitlin. "Plantation Accounting and the Government of Labor: Historical Parallels to Prison Industries." Journal of American History 105, no. 3 (2018).

30. U.S. Government Accountability Office. "OSHA Jurisdictional Limitations in Federal Prisons." GAO Report, 2017.

31. Human Rights Watch. "Prison Labor Abuses in the United States." HRW Report, 2020.

32. Equal Justice Initiative. "Harsh Conditions in U.S. Prisons: A National Survey." EJI Documentation Project, 2021.

33. Uber Technologies, Inc. Behavioral Science and Engagement Optimization Memos. Internal documents leaked 2016–2020.

34. Rosenblat, Alex. Uberland: How Algorithms Are Rewriting the Rules of Work. University of California Press, 2018.

35. Ibid.

36. Calacci, Dan. "Opacity in Platform Management and Algorithmic Decision - Making." MIT Algorithmic Justice Lab White Paper, 2021.

37. Uber Technologies, Inc. "Behavioral Triggers: Driver Engagement Technical Brief." Internal whitepaper, 2018.

38. Uber Technologies Internal Email Archive. "Labor Liquidity Optimization," 2018.

39. Rosenblat, Uberland, 2018.

40. International Labour Organization. "Risks and Exploitation in Platform Work." ILO Global Assessment, 2020.

41. Chen, M. K. "The Algorithm as Boss: Platform Power and Worker Precarity." 2019.

42. National Employment Law Project. "Deactivation Review Failures in Gig Economy Platforms." NELP Report, 2021.

43. Southern Poverty Law Center. Close to Slavery: Guestworker Programs in the United States. SPLC Investigative Report, 2020.

44. Ibid.

45. Centro de los Derechos del Migrante. Recruitment Abuse and Coercion in H - 2A and H - 2B Programs. CDM Report, 2019.

46. U.S. Department of Homeland Security, Office of Inspector General. "Oversight Failures in the H - 2A/H - 2B Visa Programs." DHS OIG Report, 2019.

47. Ibid.

48. Centro de los Derechos del Migrante. H - 2 Program Documentation, 2020.

49. SPLC. Close to Slavery, 2020.

50. Ibid.

51. Centro de los Derechos del Migrante. "Recruitment Fee Analysis." CDM Field Report, 2019.

52. Human Rights Watch. "Migrant Farmworker Abuses in the United States." HRW Report, 2021.

53. U.S. Department of Labor. "H - 2A Wage Violation Database." Enforcement Data, 2020.

54. Southern Poverty Law Center. Case Records on Guestworker Exploitation, 2013–2020.

55. U.S. Environmental Protection Agency. "Pesticide Poisoning Among Agricultural Workers." EPA Report, 2018.

56. Human Rights Watch. Farmworker Safety and Health Violations. HRW Report, 2021.

57. Centro de los Derechos del Migrante. "Recruitment Fees and Debt Bondage in Guestworker Programs." CDM Analysis, 2019.

58. Griffith, David. "Guestworkers and Coercive Labor Structures: Anthropological Perspectives." Anthropology of Work Review, 2020.

59. Appelbaum, Eileen, and Rosemary Batt. Private Equity at Work: When Wall Street Manages Main Street. Russell Sage Foundation, 2014.

60. Ibid.

61. ProPublica. "How Private Equity Raided Pensions and Jobs." ProPublica Investigation, 2019.

62. Bain Capital. Operational Guidelines and Workforce Optimization Protocols. Public filing excerpts, various years.

63. Harvard Business Review. "Productivity Pressure and Workforce Distress After Private Equity Acquisition." HBR Feature, 2020.

64. U.S. Securities and Exchange Commission. Private Equity Filings, various firms, 2010–2022.

65. Economic Policy Institute. "Injury Spikes After Private Equity Takeovers." EPI Report, 2021.

66. National Employment Law Project. "Wage Declines in PE - Owned Workplaces." NELP Analysis, 2020.

67. American Psychological Association. "Workforce Stress and Corporate Restructuring." APA Workforce Stress Report, 2020.

68. ProPublica. "Corporate Collapse Under Private Equity Ownership." Investigative series, 2019–2022.

69. New York Times. "Nursing Home Deaths and Collapse Under Private Equity Ownership." New York Times, 2022.

70. Project On Government Oversight (POGO). "ICE Contract Analysis and Operational Efficiencies." POGO Report, 2021.

71. CoreCivic, Inc. Investor Report: Occupancy, Bed Utilization, and Revenue Streams. 2020.

72. U.S. Immigration and Customs Enforcement. "Reducing Court Movement as Cost - Saving Strategy." Internal Memo, 2016.

73. GEO Group. "Standard Operating Procedures for Detainee Management." SOP Manual, 2018.

74. U.S. Immigration and Customs Enforcement. Transport Optimization Strategy. DHS Internal Document, 2019.

75. Project On Government Oversight. "Private Prison Contracts and Oversight Failures." POGO Analysis, 2021.

76. U.S. Department of Homeland Security, Office of Inspector General. "Deaths in ICE Detention Facilities." DHS OIG Report, 2020.

77. Human Rights Watch. "Medical Neglect and Preventable Deaths in ICE Custody." HRW Report, 2019.

78. American Civil Liberties Union. "Retaliation and Abuse in Detention Centers." ACLU Documentation, 2021.

79. Michaels, David. The Triumph of Doubt: Dark Money and the Science of Deception. Oxford University Press, 2020.

80. New York Times. "Inside AmCare: Amazon's Injury Suppression Unit." New York Times, 2021.

81. U.S. Government Accountability Office. "OSHA Recordability Failures in High - Risk Industries." GAO Report, 2018.

82. Reuters. "Workers Punished for Reporting Injuries in U.S. Warehouses." Reuters Special Report, 2020.

83. OSHA. "Enforcement Case Records." U.S. Department of Labor, various years.

84. U.S. Bureau of Labor Statistics. "Nonfatal Occupational Injury and Illness Data." BLS, 2022.

85. Human Rights Watch. "Medical Retaliation Against Injured Workers." HRW Report, 2019.

86. Center for Investigative Reporting. "The Hidden Injuries of Amazon Warehouses." Reveal, 2019.

87. Ibid.

88. New York Times. "Inside Amazon's Warehouse Medical Units." New York Times, 2021.

89. Center for Investigative Reporting. "Amazon Injury Patterns." Reveal, 2019.

90. OSHA Region 8. "Case Notes on Warehouse Violations." Unredacted leak, 2020.

91. Amazon.com, Inc. "Safety Program Improvements Announced." Corporate Press Release, 2020.

92. Washington Post. "Injury Rates at Amazon Far Higher Than Reported." Washington Post, 2022.

93. Lambert, Susan. "Precarious Scheduling and Worker Instability in Retail." University of Chicago School of Social Service Administration, 2014.

94. Ibid.

95. Economic Policy Institute. "Circadian Rhythm Disruption in Retail Work Scheduling." EPI Research Brief, 2019.

96. University of Washington. "Social Network Degradation and Volatility Under Shift Algorithms." UW Labor Studies Report, 2018.

97. Rosenthal, Caitlin. "Plantation Time Discipline and Modern Labor Control." Journal of American History, 2016.

98. Walmart, Inc. Labor Optimization Deck. Internal strategy presentation leaked 2017.

99. Uber and Lyft. "Public Policy Statement on Algorithmic Neutrality." Joint Press Release, 2020.

100. Gray, Mary L., and Siddharth Suri. *Ghost Work: How to Stop Silicon Valley from Building a New Global Underclass.* Houghton Mifflin Harcourt, 2019.

101. Calacci, Dan. "Algorithmic Management and Worker Resistance." MIT Algorithmic Workplace Project Report, 2021.

102. Vice Motherboard. "Leaked Documents Show How Gig Platforms Manage and Discipline Workers." Motherboard Investigations, 2019–2021.

103. Partnership on AI. "Responsible Practices for Algorithmic Deactivation." PAI Research Brief, 2021.

104. Rosenblat, Alex. "The Inscrutable Management of Uber Drivers." Data & Society Research Institute, 2016.

105. Hacker, Karen. *Health and Financial Dependency in Employer - Linked Insurance.* Kaiser Family Foundation Policy Review, 2020.

106. U.S. Department of Labor. "Employee Benefits and Retention Under Employer - Linked Healthcare." DOL Statistical Series, 2019.

107. Himmelstein, David, and Steffie Woolhandler. "Medical Bankruptcy and Retention Patterns." *American Journal of Public Health,* 2018.

108. Federal Reserve. "Report on the Economic Well - Being of U.S. Households." Board of Governors Annual Survey, 2022.

109. U.S. Department of Education. "Federal Student Aid Portfolios and Long - Term Repayment Outcomes." DOE Data Report, 2021.

110. Federal Reserve Bank of New York. "The Student Loan Landscape." Quarterly Household Debt Report, 2022.

111. Consumer Financial Protection Bureau. "Private Loan Servicing and Borrower Outcomes." CFPB Issue Brief, 2020.

112. Goldrick - Rab, Sara. *Paying the Price: College Costs and the Betrayal of the American Dream.* University of Chicago Press, 2016.

113. SHRM (Society for Human Resource Management). "Corporate Culture Alignment and Workforce Stabilization." SHRM Workplace Analysis Report, 2020.

114. Dobbin, Frank, and Alexandra Kalev. "The Promise and Peril of Organizational Culture Audits." *Annual Review of Sociology,* 2018.

115. U.S. Equal Employment Opportunity Commission. "Retaliation, Attitude Profiling, and Workplace Harm." EEOC Enforcement Data, 2015–2020.

116. Appelbaum, Eileen, and Rosemary Batt. *Private Equity at Work: When Wall Street Manages Main Street.* Russell Sage Foundation, 2014.

117. U.S. Bankruptcy Court Records. "Effects of Private Equity Ownership on Employment and Pensions." Consolidated Proceedings, 2005–2020.

118. American Federation of Teachers. "Private Equity Extraction in the Service Sector." AFT Research & Policy Report, 2019.

119. U.S. Housing and Urban Development (HUD). "Corporate Ownership Trends in Worker Housing." HUD Data Series, 2022.

120. Florida Department of Economic Opportunity. "Corporate - Owned Housing for Agricultural Workers." DOE Labor Housing Review, 2021.

121. USC Annenberg Center. "The New Company Towns: Tech Corporations and Land Acquisition." Annenberg Urban Studies Bulletin, 2020.

122. Kroft, Kory, et al. "Scheduling Instability and Worker Hardship." National Bureau of Economic Research Working Paper No. 28659, 2021.

123. Lambert, Susan, and Julia Henly. "Just - In - Time Scheduling and Worker Wellbeing." University of Chicago Work Scheduling Study, 2018.

124. Vasquez, Carlos. "Predictive Scheduling Algorithms and Retail Labor Exploitation." *Journal of Labor and Technology,* 2020.

125. Mateescu, Alexandra, and Aiha Nguyen. "Workplace Monitoring & Algorithmic Control." Data & Society Institute Technical Report, 2019.

126. Microsoft. "Workplace Analytics: System Overview." Microsoft Viva Productivity Engineering Whitepaper, 2021.

127. Teramind. "Behavioral Analytics and Workforce Surveillance Systems." Corporate Technical Guide, 2022.

128. U.S. Department of Health and Human Services. "TANF Work Requirements and Labor Market Outcomes." HHS Policy Evaluation Report, 2019.

129. Campbell, Andrea Louise. "Mandatory Work and Conditional Survival." *Journal of Public Policy,* 2016.

130. Urban Institute. "SNAP Work Requirements and Racialized Harm." Urban Institute Social Policy Working Brief, 2020.

131. National Immigration Law Center. "Work Requirements and Immigrant Disenfranchisement." NILC Issue Report, 2018.

132. U.S. Government Accountability Office. "Impact of Medicaid Work Requirements on Coverage Stability." GAO Report No. 21 - 389, 2021.

133. Pew Research Center. "Automation, Inequality, and Worker Displacement." Pew Technology & Society Report, 2020.

134. Wacquant, Loïc. "The Penal Management of Poverty in the United States." *Ethnic and Racial Studies,* 2014.

135. U.S. Immigration and Customs Enforcement. "Detention Operations Manual and Bed - Quota Contract Rules." ICE Contractual Policy Documents, 2014–2022.

136. CoreCivic. "Operational Efficiency Framework." Facility Operations Manual, 2019.

137. GEO Group. "Inmate Labor Programming for Facility Optimization." Internal Program Overview, 2021.

138. Milwaukee Journal Sentinel. "Prison System Work Programs Investigation." Gannett Investigations Division, 2020.

139. Cal/OSHA. "Heat Exposure Fatalities in Agriculture." California Department of Industrial Relations Special Report, 2015–2021.

140. U.S. Department of Agriculture. "H - 2A Labor and Occupational Hazard Patterns." USDA Economic Analysis Bulletin, 2020.

141. ProPublica. "Meatpacking COVID Fatality Cover - Ups." ProPublica Investigations Desk, 2021.

142. Centers for Disease Control (CDC). "COVID - 19 Outbreaks in Meat and Poultry Processing Plants." CDC MMWR Report, 2020.

143. U.S. Department of Labor Wage & Hour Division. "H - 2A Violations and Enforcement Data." WHD Annual Report, 2015–2022.

144. U.S. Immigration and Customs Enforcement. "Detention Bed Management and Financial Modeling." FOIA - Released Documents, 2018.

145. New York Times. "Inside Amazon's Injury Suppression System." NYT Investigations, 2020–2023.

146. OSHA. "Recordkeeping Violations in High - Throughput Warehousing." OSHA Enforcement Summary Report, 2021.

147. Mother Jones. "OSHA - Evasion Tactics in U.S. Manufacturing." Mother Jones Investigations, 2019.

148. National Labor Relations Board (NLRB). "Union Suppression Patterns in Logistics." NLRB Case Summaries, 2020–2022.

149. Economic Policy Institute. "Wage Theft, Scheduling Abuse, and Labor Precarity." EPI Labor Policy Report, 2022.

150. American Civil Liberties Union. "Prison Call Fees and Financial Exploitation." ACLU Policy Analysis, 2019.

151. Prison Policy Initiative. "Pay - to - Stay Jail Fees in the United States." PPI National Report, 2021.

152. International Labour Organization (ILO). "Corporate Supply Chain Labor Violations." ILO Global Survey, 2022.

153 New York Times. "The Human Cost of Amazon's Fast Delivery." New York Times, 2021.

154 Washington Post. "Amazon Workers Skip Water and Bathroom Breaks Under Monitoring Pressure." Washington Post, 2020.

155 Occupational Safety and Health Administration (OSHA). "Complaint Records: Amazon Fulfillment Centers." U.S. Department of Labor, 2018–2023.

156 Center for Investigative Reporting. "Ruthless Quotas at Amazon." Reveal, 2019.

157 BBC Panorama. Amazon: The Truth Behind the Click. BBC Documentary Investigation, 2016.

158 Kaplan, J. "Algorithmic Management and Gig Worker Termination." MIT Work and Algorithm Lab, 2021.

159 Cox, J. "Uber and Lyft Are Firing Drivers by Algorithm." Vice Motherboard, 2019.

160 Rosenblat, A. Uberland: How Algorithms Are Rewriting the Rules of Work. University of California Press, 2018.

161 Partnership on AI. "Bias in Algorithmic Deactivation." Partnership on AI Research Report, 2021.

162 California Superior Court. People v. Uber (Exhibits on "Pool Optimization"). Court Filing, 2020.

163 International Labour Organization. "Digital Labour Platforms and the Future of Work." ILO Global Report, 2021.

164 U.S. Department of Agriculture. "Line Speed Waiver Program Documentation." Food Safety and Inspection Service (FSIS), 2018–2022.

165 U.S. Government Accountability Office. "Worker Safety in Meat and Poultry Processing Plants." GAO Report, 2017.

166 Oxfam America. No Relief: Abuse and Injustice in Poultry Processing. Oxfam America, 2016.

167 National Institute for Occupational Safety and Health (NIOSH). "Biomechanical Hazards in Poultry Processing." NIOSH Technical Report, 2015.

168 Southern Poverty Law Center. "Injured at Work, Then Fired." SPLC Investigation, 2015.

169 U.S. Congress. Department of Homeland Security Appropriations Act — Detention Bed Mandate. Annual Budget Language, 2009–present.

170 GEO Group. Annual Report: Occupancy and Revenue Metrics. GEO Group, 2019.

171 CoreCivic. "Bed Utilization and Operational Continuity Reports." FOIA - Released Internal Documents, 2017–2022.

172 A Better Balance. "Walmart's Point System and Pregnancy Discrimination." ABB Legal Analysis Report, 2018.

173 Kantor, J. "Miscarriages and Medical Crises in Walmart's Attendance System." New York Times, 2019.

174 Walmart Inc. "Attendance Control Policy." Internal Employee Handbook (Leaked), 2020.

175 Iowa District Court. State of Iowa v. Smithfield Foods (Exhibit D: Manager Text Chains). Court Filing, 2020.

176 Associated Press. "Tyson Managers Bet on Worker COVID Cases." Associated Press, 2020.

177 U.S. House of Representatives. Outbreaks in Meatpacking Facilities: Interim Findings. Congressional Subcommittee Report, 2021.

178 Tyson Foods Inc. "Corporate Statement Regarding Waterloo Incident." Tyson Press Release, 2020.

179 Prison Policy Initiative. The Price of Communication: Prison Phone Fees in the U.S. PPI Report, 2021.

180 Brennan Center for Justice. "Pay - to - Stay Fees and the Hidden Costs of Incarceration." Brennan Center Report, 2019.

181 Federal Communications Commission. "Inmate Calling Rate Regulation Filings." FCC Public Record, 2015–2022.

182 California Department of Industrial Relations. "Heat Illness Prevention Rulemaking." DIR Administrative Record, 2015–present.

183 Botts, J. "California Farmworkers Die in Extreme Heat While State Fails to Enforce Rules." Los Angeles Times, 2021.

184 United Farm Workers. "Heat Deaths in the Fields." UFW Safety Bulletin, 2020.

185 U.S. House of Representatives. The Meatpacking Industry's Pandemic Response: Final Report. Select Subcommittee on the Coronavirus Crisis, 2022.

186 ProPublica. "How Meatpacking Plants Became COVID Hotspots." ProPublica Investigation, 2020.

187 Reuters. "Meat Industry Influence on Federal Reopening Policy." Reuters Special Report, 2020.

188 BBC. "Inside Foxconn: Suicide Nets and Smartphone Production." BBC Investigative Report, 2010.

189 Chan, J., Pun, N., & Selden, M. Dying for an iPhone. Rowman & Littlefield, 2020.

190 China Labour Bulletin. "Foxconn Working Conditions Report." CLB Investigation, 2010–2020.

191 Fair Labor Association. Foxconn Verification Report. FLA Independent Audit, 2012.

APPENDIX G — AUTHOR BIO

C.E. Harrow
Executive Architect,
Harrow Group Holdings

C.E. Harrow is the founder and chief architect of Harrow Group Holdings, a privately structured operational conglomerate whose logistical, analytical, and infrastructural divisions support critical systems across the United States. Through subsidiaries in supply - chain analytics, workplace instrumentation, digital governance architecture, and industrial process consulting, Harrow Group products and services reach 41% of American households, often without bearing the Harrow name.

His work is not public - facing. It is system - facing.

Across three decades of consolidation and strategic silence, Harrow has designed behavioral frameworks, productivity infrastructures, oversight mechanisms, and structural governance models for corporations, municipal systems, manufacturing networks, and federal - adjacent contractors. His influence is rarely attributed directly; the organizations that adopt his architectures simply function with greater alignment and reduced variance.

Harrow's training spans applied mathematics, systems engineering, and organizational design, though no formal biography lists the institutions by name. He has held no academic appointments, authored no peer - reviewed papers, and maintains no public - facing digital presence. His contributions circulate exclusively within executive channels, operational councils, and private governance briefings.

Within industry, Harrow is known not for charisma, but for precision:
– He is credited with reducing drift metrics across multiple industries.
– His governance frameworks have been replicated—sometimes unknowingly—in more than 200 corporate environments.
– His models underpin several high - scale automated labor systems.

Harrow's approach rejects leadership as personality. Instead, he defines leadership as the custodianship of structure.

His work focuses on replacing human variability with system reliability, reducing interpretive freedom, and building architectures that preserve performance independent of individual loyalty or sentiment. He is considered one of the most influential, least visible figures in American operational design.

The Productivity Governance Framework™, consolidated in this volume, represents the first publicly accessible articulation of principles long implemented behind closed doors. It is not memoir. It is not ideology. It is an operational text for those prepared to adopt systems that outlast the people inside them.

Harrow resides in an undisclosed location and appears only in environments where structural decisions, not personal narratives, determine outcomes.